# Ontario's
# Secret
# Landscapes

# Ontario's Secret Landscapes

### 50 More Visits to Unusual Ontario

*Ron Brown*

Cataloguing in Publication Data

Brown, Ron 1945-
 Ontario's secret landscapes

ISBN 1-55046-298-9

1. Ontario - Guidebooks.
2. Curiosities and wonders - Ontario - Guidebooks.
I. Title.

FC3057.B77 1999   917.304'4   C99-930276-0
F1057.7.B775 1999

03 02 01 00 99   1 2 3 4 5


Published in 1999 by
Boston Mills Press
132 Main Street
Erin, Ontario  N0B 1T0
Tel 519-833-2407
Fax 519-833-2195
e-mail books@boston-mills.on.ca
www.boston-mills.on.ca

An affiliate of
Stoddart Publishing Co. Limited
34 Lesmill Road
Toronto, Ontario, Canada
M3B 2T6
Tel 416-445-3333
Fax 416-445-5967
e-mail gdsinc@genpub.com

Distributed in Canada by
General Distribution Services Limited
325 Humber College Boulevard
Toronto, Canada M9W 7C3
Orders 1-800-387-0141 Ontario & Quebec
Orders 1-800-387-0172 NW Ontario & Other Provinces
e-mail customer.service@ccmailgw.genpub.com
EDI Canadian Telebook S1150391

Distributed in the United States by
General Distribution Services Inc.
85 River Rock Drive, Suite 202
Buffalo, New York 14207-2170
Toll-free 1-800-805-1083
Toll-free fax 1-800-481-6207
e-mail gdsinc@genpub.com
www.genpub.com
PUBNET 6307949


Design by Joseph Gisini, Andrew Smith Graphics Inc.
Printed in Canada


*Boston Mills Press gratefully acknowledges the Canada Council for the Arts, the Government of Canada through the Book Publishing Industry Development Program (BPIDP), and the Ontario Arts Council for their support of our publishing program.*

*This volume is dedicated
to my Gang:
June, Jeri and Ria.*

# Contents

# Ontario's Most Unusual Buildings

# Amazing Monuments

# Hidden Valleys

# Nature's Puzzles

# Getting it Right

# Transport to the Past

# Mining Days

# Introduction

As urban Ontario sprawls further into the vanishing countryside, its residents spend more time in their cars. Even basic conveniences require a car. Big box shopping centres are several kilometres apart. Work places are in distant suburbs where public transit is an after-thought. Traffic congestion leads to gridlock and road rage.

But get out of the car and you can explore an Ontario few realize exists. Down some side road, or behind a bush, or perhaps across a lake, you will find strange and unusual features.

These features tell many of the stories of this province. Unusual rock formations unveil the forces of nature sculpting a wonderland of caverns, chasms and strange shapes. Ruins recount mistakes and failed dreams. Monuments to unheralded heroes and fascinating buildings reveal forgotten chapters in history. Past transportation, such as railroads, might even offer a solution to today's travel headaches.

This book is a guide to unusual features. *Secret Landscapes* continues the series that began with *50 Unusual Things to See in Ontario*, and its companion volume, *50 Even More Unusual Things to See in Ontario*. I hope Ontario residents will slow down long enough to see and appreciate Ontario's secret landscapes.

# Pre-Historic
# Puzzles

# 1

# Those Perplexing
##                   Pukaskwa Pits

Among the most unusual of Ontario's places pre-date written history. Prehistoric inhabitants left behind mounds, pits, and paintings. They filled crucial roles in their lives, but left question marks for a modern generation. Some of these riddles are solved. Yet many remain unanswered.

What makes our First Nations' heritage so mysterious is the lack of written history. European conquerors, ignorant about the native's "savage" ways, including language, stifled the oral tradition. Today's generation has difficulty understanding the paintings, the petroglyphs, or the mysterious pukaskwa pits.

Found primarily around the shores of Lake Superior, pukaskwa pits (pronounced puk-a-saw) are man-made excavations dug into boulder beaches formed when the lake waters were about 30 metres higher than they are today. The conical pits are two or three metres across with excavated stones piled protectively around the rim. Although clearly man-made, the lack of other evidence of human occupation, such as burial mounds, dumps or habitation areas, heightens their mystery. Archaeologists have found only bits of pottery, flints, and caribou bones, suggesting the use of the pits was likely short-term.

One theory suggests they were vision pits. Young men of each tribe isolated themselves until the spirit of the animal that guided their lives visited them. Others speculate the pits were shelters from the storm-tossed waters of the lake during the peak of the fur trade. Their location close to the water, but away from the waves, makes excellent shelters for canoeists. Huddled inside, one is protected from the cold winds while soaking up the sun. Some of the larger pits appear to have had hearths and possibly protective coverings.

The greatest concentration of pukaskwa pits is found along the northeast shore of Lake Superior. More than 250 are protected in Pukaskwa National Park. Because they can be easily altered, or even destroyed by accident or carelessness, their exact locations are not published.

These unexplained excavations are found throughout Ontario.

Pukaskwa Park epitomizes northern Ontario. The province's highest mountain peak is the 640-metre high Tip Top Mountain. Wild rivers plunge through steep canyons. Dense forests cloak the soaring hillsides. Waves hurl themselves against a rocky shore with cliffs as high as 300 metres above the grey waters.

The park entrances many visitors with awe-inspiring scenery and sheer isolation. Like early dwellers, even modern visitors might find spiritual power here.

The park is accessed from Highway 17 by following Highway 627 through Heron Bay. Here you find the Friends of Pukaskwa store. From the campground and visitor centre, a 60-kilometre hiking trail leads along the coast to its end at Hattie Bay. A well-travelled canoe route follows the shore with campsites at several locations.

Although the locations of the mystery pits are not given, those who hike or canoe the shoreline of the park will quickly find a few of these mysterious holes and ponder their origin.

# 2

# Thornbury's
# Mystery Mound

For years experts remained skeptical over the presence of the Norse in Canada. Today, the L'Anse Aux Meadows Viking village in Newfoundland has become an UNESCO World Heritage Site. Despite skepticism, some writers now claim Celts, Irish monks, or a people called Albans might even have preceded the Norse to Canada's shores.

Stone carvings discovered in Newfoundland that resemble Celtic script have inspired many debates. Farley Mowat advances another controversial theory that a group of indigenous Scots, whom he calls Albans, left evidence of habitation in Canada's Arctic.

How can we explain the puzzling prehistoric man-made mound on a hill high above Thornbury? The smooth round shape is not consistent with any natural formation. The mound consists of red clay and measures 10 metres high, 80 metres in diameter and is topped by a boulder with a line of crystal pointing due north.

Ontario's prehistoric aboriginals constructed burial mounds. The electrical anomalies detected by ground probing radar are strikingly consistent with similar anomalies found in known Celtic burial mounds in Ireland and Switzerland. One theory claims Bronze Age European Celts sailed to North America in search of copper, the most popular trading item among Great Lakes natives.

Did ancient Celtic traders create this mound?

But with no written records from those dark times, the mystery may never be solved.

To confound matters further, Ontario has other mounds. Bruce Trail hikers in the vicinity of Blue Mountain, Creemore, the Hockley Valley and the Forks of the Credit have noticed similar shapes.

The mound can be seen if you follow the Collingwood St. Vincent Town Line Road from Highway 26 just west of Thornbury. The mound sits on top of the west wall of the Beaver Valley a few metres northwest of the intersection of Collingview Street and Number 7 Sideroad.

One final note. The view from the mound extends east across the Beaver Valley to the Blue Mountain location of the next mound. Could these have been Celtic signal towers or navigational guides? The mystery deepens.

# 3

# Ontario's Serpent Mounds

Ironically, the strongest visual evidence of Ontario's native heritage deals not with life but with death. Usually, places where Ontario's prehistoric peoples lived are seldom discernible to any but the trained archaeologist. Yet where they died can have prominent physical features.

Take, for example, Rice Lake's unusual serpent mound. Although no other such mounds exist elsewhere in Canada, burial mounds in the shape of giant snakes are common in the U.S. Ohio Valley.

The mound, on the north shore of Rice Lake, is two metres high, eight metres wide, and a twisting 60 metres long. Several other burial mounds with common oval shape surround it. An example of the latter exists at Tabor Hill Park in Scarborough, uncovered when the site was being prepared for housing. Archaeologists cannot decide whether the serpent mound was intended to resemble a snake because it lacks a head. Or was it an ordinary mound somehow extended?

Following the retreat of the glaciers around 20,000 years ago, this arctic-like area abounded in caribou, bison, and possibly even mammoth. The first inhabitants were nomadic. As the climate warmed, forests covered the tundra bringing smaller game like deer and rabbits. Berries and root crops became part of the staple diet. The time of the nomads was about to end.

Around 1000 BC, the mound building culture entered the area. Originating in the Ohio Valley, it gradually made its way into Ontario, culminating in the collection of mounds on Rice Lake. No evidence suggests this was a village site. The absence of bones from winter game suggests it was a summer gathering place for trading, rice harvesting, and burials.

Around 500 AD a revolutionary new way of life arrived. Corn and squash replaced hunting and gathering. Permanent villages were built with longhouses surrounded by palisades. Pits instead of mounds were used for burials. The presence of burial pits north of the mounds and a habitation area west of them confirms the existence of the new life style. Consecutive harvests eventually leached the soil so the inhabitants moved to more fertile grounds.

The arrival of the Europeans in the late 18th and early 19th century ended to that way of life. First Nations peoples were moved onto reserves. A logging dam near the outlet to Rice Lake flooded the rice beds and a way of life ended forever.

Today the mounds are part of Serpent Mounds Park. Here these long vanished cultures and customs are interpreted for a modern world.

This serpentine ridge is the legacy of a vanished culture that practised mound burials.

# Ontario's Richness of Ruins

# 4

# Fort St. Joseph

In Europe, great pride is taken in ruins. Ruins directly link with the mysterious past. The builders and inhabitants touched these rocks and walls. Ontario slowly recognizes the value of its ruins. A few manage to survive to give visitors a tantalizing hint of the past.

From the days of the earliest fur traders to the Fenian raids of the 1860s Ontario needed defending. The forts ranged from a cabin or two within a crude stockade, like the Willow Creek Depot, up to the massive stone towers, walls and ramparts of Fort Henry.

A few restored forts are popular tourist attractions. Fort George at Niagara-on-the-Lake, Fort Wellington near Prescott, Fort Erie, Fort Henry at Kingston, or Fort Malden at Amherstburg are among the regular stops on Ontario's busy tourist circuit. But the old forts provide the truest link with the past.

Some, like Fort Lacloche on the North Channel of Lake Huron, are nearly impossible to locate. At Fort St. Joseph the ruins provide visitors with an insight into the difficult life of the inhabitants.

Forced by the treaty that ended the American Revolution to cede the strategic Fort Michilimackinac, the British needed a fort to defend the western fur trade routes. In 1796, at the entrance to the St. Mary River, which drains Lake Superior into Lake Huron, they built Fort St. Joseph.

As the clouds of war approached again in 1812, the garrison set

The excavated ruins of remote Fort St. Joseph are the original and only slightly altered foundations of an early fort.

out from the fort, accompanied by warriors from the Ojibway and Ottawa tribes, and recaptured Fort Michilimackinac. St. Joseph was undefended. Unable to retake their own fort, the Americans burned the abandoned St. Joseph. Rather than rebuild, the British relocated to Drummond Island and then to Penetanguishene. The ruins at Fort St. Joseph remain today to give visitors a touch of Canada's military past.

From the visitor centre, where a video depicts life at the fort, a path leads to the site. The ramparts are just mounds in a field. Within the palisades lie the foundations of the bake house, block house, kitchen, and stores building.

The trail then leads down to the site of the military wharf and

The bake house is one of Fort St. Joe's more extensive ruins.

the civilian village that stood nearby. The foundations of a pair of cabins and a blacksmith shop have been identified. East of the visitor centre in the old military cemetery, the crosses are recent additions to mark the sites of known graves. From the fort, the view extends across the channel of the river and beyond to the open waters of Lake Huron. The vista has little changed from the days when the soldiers of the garrison scoured the horizon for the sails of enemy ships.

# 5

# Lake Superior's Prisoner of War Camps

One of the Second World War's great escapes took place, not in occupied Europe, but on the shores of Lake Superior. The relics of it remain to this day.

As the allies made incursions into the German front during the dark days of the war, Prisoner of War camps were needed. The north shore of Lake Superior was ideal. The area was remote, surrounded by vast areas of steep terrain and thick forests, yet accessible from the CPR's Lake Superior main line.

Two of these camps, at Angler and Neys, were close together. During the war, POW camps were carefully segregated. Camps were for prisoners considered pro-Nazi, for anti-Nazis, for commissioned officers, for merchant seamen, and to Canada's shame, for Japanese-Canadians uprooted from the coast of BC.

The pro-Nazi camp at Neys was set aside for elite German officers. Housed in 27 buildings, and surrounded by three sets of barbed wire, they were carefully watched over from four guard towers. Although a tunnel was dug, no one escaped. Some claim this was because the prisoners preferred to operate a secret still. With smuggled canned fruit and sugar the Germans concocted an effective home-brewed whisky. One inspection revealed a guard passed out on the floor surrounded by eight drunken Germans, happily singing at the top of their lungs.

The steps of the officers' mess when it was a German prisoner of war camp.

But increased security followed a massive escape from a neighbouring camp. Five miles west of Marathon stood the Angler POW camp. Much larger than Neys, it housed over 1,000 enlisted German soldiers in 75 buildings. They engineered one of the most sophisticated escape efforts of the war.

In January of 1941, the Germans were still optimistic that the war would go their way. The Germans immediately planned their escape. Using spoons and pans lifted from the kitchen, they tunneled under five of the barracks and beneath the exterior fence. The elaborate ploy involved stolen maps, a two-way radio disguised as a model ship, and tunnel noise covered up by musical instruments.

By April all was ready. More than 80 Germans lined up at the tunnel entrance equipped with stolen rations. As they made their way through the tunnel, one tripped over the makeshift shovels, and alerted the guards. Only 28 made it out. But terrible conditions awaited them. Plunging temperatures and raging blizzards turned their freedom into a nightmare. Within two days, half were recaptured freezing and lost in the nearby woods. Four others lasted a week. Five were discovered in a railway shack and shot. Two boarded a slow moving freight train and ended up in Alberta. But they were discovered and sent back to the camp.

The following year the Germans were moved out and Japanese-Canadian internees moved in. After the war the camp was disassembled completely. Neys was a prison farm for a few years before it was dismantled.

While no structures stand from those dark war days, the two sites contain a number of intriguing vestiges. At Angler visitors can

At Neys Provincial Park is a stone sidewalk built by German prisoners of war.

see the remains of the barbed wire fences, utensils, rusting vehicles, and various foundations, as well as the prison cemetery. The site of Neys camp lies within Neys Provincial Park. During the summer interpretive walks lead park visitors to the camp remains. The foundations of guard towers and water tanks, a cobblestone walk built by the prisoners, the cement steps that led to the officers' mess, and the imprint of an unused escape tunnel can be seen.

Angler is south off Highway 17 about eight kilometres west of Marathon to the east of Angler Creek. From here it is 20 minutes along a rough road suitable only for four-wheel drive vehicles. The POW campsite lies past the end of the road across a grassy area and over a creek. The Neys camp is located in the provincial park 18 kilometres further west along Highway 17.

# 6

# The Secret
## of Camp X

While many of the Second World War's great secrets have been declassified only in recent years, Camp X, near Ajax on Lake Ontario, has long been known as one of the war's top spy training centre.

Cloak and dagger movies and spy thrillers like the James Bond books conjure images of stealth, danger, and sultry temptresses. In reality, undercover work was humdrum. Most espionage work censored mail, broke letter codes or forged diplomatic documents.

The man in charge of Camp X was nicknamed "Intrepid." In real life he was William (later Sir William) Stephenson. Born in Winnipeg, the decorated World War One flying ace was put in charge of British counter-espionage during the Second World War. Stephenson was the subject of several best-selling books. *A Man Called Intrepid,* by William Stevenson is the best known.

Another writer trained in Camp X wrote a series of spy books. That author was Ian Fleming. His hero was the suave super-spy James Bond.

The camp consisted of two components. The Special Training School, or STS 103, focused on spy training. A more secret activity, code-named Hydra, involved top secret messages sent between Canada and the United States.

After the war, Camp X continued as a government communications centre until 1969. The buildings were then dismantled and the land sold to the Town of Whitby. Stephenson retired to Bermuda.

In 1984, the field became "Intrepid Park" and a large monument was erected to commemorate those who worked in Camp X. On the base of the monument photographs and text depict the story of the camp and its contribution to the Allied victory. From the monument, trails lead to an isolated beach on the Lake Ontario where, no doubt, a few clandestine arrivals and departures occurred. Above the base, four flags flap in the breeze. The flags are an anachronism in an otherwise featureless field.

Surrounded by industries, the little manicured park sits on Boundary Road in Ajax at the point where it bends east to become Phillip Murray Avenue.

Other than the monument, little remains of Camp X, the top secret war facility where James Bond was born in the mind of author Ian Fleming.

# 7

# The Missing Town

Across Ontario, towns were mapped out. Some remained small, some boomed, some never made it off the paper. But rarely were the sidewalks, hydrants, and roads built only to remain empty and unused.

Windsor, Ontario, grew in a most unusual way. While most towns started small, perhaps around a mill site or a port, and then expanded outward, Windsor came about as an amalgamation of planned company towns. Walkerville developed around Hiram Walker's whiskey distillery. Their neighbour, Ford City, was incorporated in 1913 as a residential community for the company's automotive plant.

Then there was Ojibway.

Ojibway differed from Walkerville and Ford City. While these predecessors used a traditional grid network of streets, Ojibway represented the latest in town planning. Streets radiated outward from three central squares, while a four-lane expressway linked it with Windsor, then seven kilometres away.

Ojibway was a 1,800-acre company town for the American Canadian Steel Corporation. Construction started during World War One and continued into the 1920s. Objections, however, from Canadian steel producers, the effects of the depression, and huge underground salt deposits beneath the proposed streets, halted the project.

A sidewalk in the woods of missing Ojibway.

Although a few industrial buildings were completed, and the roads and sidewalks built, the population remained below 100. During the intervening years, grass and weeds reclaimed the streets and sidewalks. Forests re-grew on the undeveloped area. By the 1960s, Ojibway had earned a distinction as Canada's smallest organized municipality.

Following Ojibway's annexation to Windsor in 1966, suburban growth spread to the old townsite. New housing appeared on some of the original streets. A racetrack was built in the middle of the town. But much remained undeveloped. Grandly named streets like

Broadview and Ojibway Parkway curved past open fields where rusting hydrants poked above the tall grasses. Part of the planned four-lane express route became a local lane named Sandwich Street. Cement sidewalks cut straight through mature woodlots.

To reach the forest with the sidewalk, follow Normandy Street east from Malden. The doglegs in the dirt road following Ellis Street and Washington Blvd. represent the proposed streets that now lead only through the woods. Cement sidewalks line these dirt lanes and at regular intervals cut straight into the forests.

Many of Ontario's communities have a strange history, but none so strange as Ojibway, the missing town.

# 8

# Ontario's First
## Native Town

On the north bank of the Thames River near London is the site of one of Ontario's first permanent native villages. Fairfield was chosen by Moravian missionaries anxious to lead a band of Delaware Indians from persecutions in post-revolutionary U.S. In 1792 they arrived on the banks of the Thames River. On a land grant from the British, they built Fairfield. The village was intended to be permanent. Along its main street were a two-storey church, two schools, a few shops, and 50 houses.

But they could not escape the brutality of the Americans. In 1813, an invading army launched a series of devastating raids along the shore of Lake Erie and up the Thames River. At the Battle of Moraviantown, they drove back the British, killed the popular chief Tecumseh, and burned Fairfield. After seeking safety in Burlington until the war ended, the Moravians brought the group back. This time they went to the opposite shore of the Thames where they established New Fairfield. Their descendants occupy the location to this day.

Old Fairfield was forgotten by all except noted archaeologist Wilfred Jury. Between 1942 and 1944, he excavated the site. Then a philanthropist named W.A. McGeachy purchased it. Thanks to them the location is now preserved as part of a United Church of Canada museum.

Because a detailed village plan was drawn at the time of settlement, the original village has been accurately depicted showing the locations of 40 houses along the village's main street. Even the names of the former inhabitants are displayed where their simple log homes once stood.

The map is displayed in the small museum, along with artifacts from the original village. A small woodlot across the road to the north represents the site of the original cemetery where more than 120 of the residents once lay buried. Across the river to the south, the steeple of the New Fairfield church rises above the trees.

The site of Old Fairfield is on former Highway 2 between Wardsville and Bothwell.

A gravel pathway represents the main street of Old Fairfield.

# 9

# The Castles
## of the Cuesta

One of Ontario's most significant natural features is the Niagara Escarpment. A 400-kilometre cuesta that extends from Queenston to Tobermory, it offers viewpoints, rare vegetation, caves, grottos and Canada's oldest trees.

Recognizing the need to preserve the integrity of the Escarpment, the Ontario government, headed by premier William Davis, set up a controversial commission in l971 to prepare a plan to guide, and, if necessary, restrict inappropriate development. Public hearings pitted the development rights proponents, developers, quarry operators, and wealthy property owners against the preservationists and the naturalists. The resulting compromise plan satisfied no one. Although the United Nations has declared the Escarpment an UNESCO world biosphere reserve, its future remains fragile.

The wealthy have long been attracted to this rare and beautiful landscape. Throughout the 19th century a number of mansions were built along its summit or in its wooded gullies. A handful survives as ruins of long-gone grandeur and faded elegance.

High on a cliff overlooking St. Catharines is the stone foundation of the mansion built in 1812 by Captain John DeCou (later changed to Decew.) During the war, it served as British army headquarters. To this building Laura Secord and a cow made that famous trek to warn Lieutenant Fitzgibbon of a pending Yankee attack.

The stone ruins of the Hermitage.

The house remained in the Decew family until 1942. Then the property was bought by the Hydro Electric Power Commission to expand the Decew generating station. Gutted by fire in 1950, the fine home was reduced to stone foundations, fireplaces, and a few walls. The ruins are located on Decew Road, a short distance east of the Mountain Mills Museum.

George Leith, however, preferred the Escarpment's wooded gully near Ancaster to a cuesta summit for his Hermitage. Son of a Scottish baronet, Leith built this elaborate mansion in 1855 as a summer home. He used stone quarried on the property. The rolling woodlands reminded him of his native Scotland where he wintered. Following a devastating fire in 1934, Leith's daughter, Eleanor, built a smaller home within the shell of the Hermitage and lived there until her death in 1942. In 1972, the Hamilton Region Conservation Authority bought the property. Accessible only by a walking trail,

The stone ruins of the Corran.

the sudden appearance of the gaunt ruins in the stillness of woodland emphasizes their haunting appeal.

James McLaren built the McLaren Castle in 1864. Overlooking the Forks of the Credit, its prominent Norman tower dominated the landscape for many miles. Following a fire in 1964, only the first floor was reconstructed. Still on private property, it can be seen from the road 600 metres south of the intersection of the 3rd Line and the 5th Sideroad about five kilometres south east of Belfountain.

North west of Osler Bluff, near Collingwood, are the ruins of Osler Castle or Konionto (Huron for "Top of the Hill") built in 1895 by a prominent lawyer named Britton Bath Osler. The elaborate 15-room mansion was never finished, and fell into disuse following Osler's death in 1901. Although inaccessible, the ruins are visible from the New Mountain Road about ten kilometres south of Collingwood.

One of the most ambitious of the Castles of the Cuesta was the Corran. Alexander McNeill built this 17-room palace in 1882 on a bluff overlooking Colpoy's Bay near Wiarton. McNeill chose the site to remind himself of the rugged beauty he had left behind in his native County Antrim, Ireland. His castle included rose gardens, an icehouse, large library and conservatory, as well as the first electrical generating plant in the area. After 1960 it fell victim to local vandals and was purchased by the North Grey Conservation Authority. The roofless ruins lie within the Spirit Rock Conservation Area on Highway 6 on the northern outskirts of Wiarton.

Of all the public bodies in Ontario, the conservation authorities have done more to preserve and celebrate a vanishing rural heritage than any other single body. Their preservation of the ruins at the Hermitage and the Corran portray the heritage of a province from a different perspective. The dreams of even the rich and famous can collapse into ruin.

**Footnote:** In 1996, the Tory government of Premier Mike Harris stripped from the conservation authorities the mandate to invest in heritage preservation. And to make sure they didn't, it removed their funding as well. The future of the castles of the cuesta, and indeed of the entire cuesta itself, is threatened by government shortsightedness such as this.

# Around Toronto

# 10

# The Mackenzie House
# and Other Ghost Stories

Haunted places abound in Toronto.

The best known is the haunting of Mackenzie House. William Lyon Mackenzie, promoter of representative government, publisher of the controversial *Colonial Advocate*, and fomenter of the 1837 rebellion, lived at 32 Bond Street from 1859 until 1861. After a long litany of ownership changes the building became a private museum in 1934. The Toronto Historical Board bought the property in 1960.

Stories of the ghost in the Mackenzie House began circulating during the late 1950s. During that time staff and live-in caretakers reported frequent noises, including a piano playing. One story claims a physical assault on a caretaker's wife. The specter was variously reported as a lady in grey or a short man in a frock. Although Mackenzie died in the house, no evidence suggests his was a troubled spirit. None of his family died in the house. The ghost's identity remains a puzzle.

One story suggests the house functioned as a bordello. One of the inmates was murdered on the third floor and her spirit seeks solace. While the Toronto Historical Board's booklet, "The Haunting of Mackenzie House" debunks the stories, they took the precaution to have the house exorcised before locating their offices on the third floor.

The haunted McKenzie House is now a museum.

Toronto's grand old City Hall has been the subject of much ghostly activity. A number of noted judges have heard noises or had their robes tugged by invisible hands. Janitors hear footsteps. Noises are routinely heard coming from old Courtroom 33, the chamber where Canada's last death sentences were handed down.

Toronto's Hockey Hall of Fame, at Yonge and Front, served as a bank between 1847 and 1983. The source of strange sounds, some say, are those of a female bank teller. She was rejected in an adulterous affair and shot herself in the staff washroom.

Staff in the Cherry Hill House Restaurant, located in an 1807 farmhouse, has reported the faces and bodies of Indians floating through the building. Archaeologists later discovered some of the blocks for the house were unceremoniously relocated from a nearby Indian burial ground.

Built in 1829, Colborne Lodge was the rural retreat for John Howard. In 1873, he donated to the City of Toronto the forested property now called High Park. For a number of years, his wife Jemima lay ill in an upstairs bedroom. She would stand at the window and look down upon her burial plot. In 1969, a patrolling police officer noticed a figure in the second story window looking out onto the grave of Lady Howard. Numerous others claim to have observed this specter, though staff at the building, now a museum, remain skeptical.

The most ghoulish Toronto ghosts are the three ladies haunting the basement hallways of the Queens Park Legislative buildings. Prior to the structure's appointment as the seat of government, the site was a lunatic asylum. Many inmates died an unhappy death. While the gowned Lady in White and the Maiden in her checkered dress are relatively benign, the "Hanging Woman," suspended from a hook in a basement hall sends shivers up the parliamentary spine. Now that's a ghost story.

# 11

# The Casa Loma Stables

Casa Loma dominates Toronto's brochures, has felt the footsteps of millions of tourists, and has been the location for dozens of movies. Toronto's best-known landmark is also its only castle.

Less well known, are the incredible Casa Loma stables. In fact, these elegant barns were finished full four years before construction on the castle even started. They are considered the most lavish on the continent.

Visitors to Toronto's most famous castle often overlook the Casa Loma stables.

Casa Loma's stable was as grand as the "castle" itself.

The castle's owner and builder was Sir Henry Pellatt. A multimillionaire, Pellatt earned his riches by building the CPR to the west. He used his earnings to build the first Canadian hydro generating station at Niagara Falls.

But he also loved the military and castles. In 1905 he purchased 25 residential lots on top of the Davenport Escarpment, and hired architect Edward James Lennox, designer of the city's most prominent buildings, including the old city hall, to build his castle. By 1914, the dream castle was complete on the outside. Huge cost overruns, however, prevented his finishing the interior. After ten years, his wife's illness, and financial ruin, forced him from it.

Yet the lesser-known stables more truly reflect the life style and the tastes of this mysterious man. Described as the most lavish anywhere on the continent, the buildings were completed in 1906, four years before the castle was even started. Inside, the stalls are of mahogany, with the horse's names spelled out in gold lettering above each. The floors were covered in Spanish tiles, laid in a herring bone pattern so that horses would not slip. Pellatt's favourite horse, named Prince, was even outfitted with a set of false teeth. Dominated by towers and turrets, the entrance is framed in white stone to contrast with the red brick of the building.

Adjoining the stables, the carriage house boasts a room larger even than the castle's main hall. Here, Pellatt stored his magnificent carriages and Toronto's first electric car. The stables and carriage are connected to the castle by an 800-foot long tunnel.

Two other buildings in the Casa Loma complex, likewise little known, are the Pellatt Lodge and the workers' homes. Built in 1905, these accommodated Pellatt and his workmen while the castle was under construction. The lodge is a two-storey residence, built of red brick, with caste iron trim, and octagonal towers. Just north of the stables is the duplex built for the workers in a style similar to both the lodge and the stables.

# 12

# The Yorkville Rock
# and Other Strange Parks

The rock is more than a billion years old, weighs 650 tonnes, and cost $300,000, yet it contains no precious metals or minerals. Plunked right in the middle of Toronto's priciest shopping district, it is known, somewhat derogatorily, as the Yorkville Rock.

In 1966, Toronto's new east-west subway slashed through the hippy haven known as Yorkville Village, a collection of coffee houses tucked into the basements of a row of 19th century homes. Although the little neighborhood evolved into an ever-pricier shopping area, the subway route had left a no-man's land on which nothing heavy could be built. For years the strip of land remained an unsightly parking lot.

Finally, in 1991, the City of Toronto, and the local business association, hired Architect Olesand Worland to create a park to fit both the context and the history of the area. Worland proposed an inner-city ecological experience. In just one city block, his park would display the ecological variety of the entire province. While the trees and the flowers presented no problem, Toronto offered nothing that resembled Ontario's most extensive landscape element, the Canadian Shield, whose hard rounded rocks are the oldest on earth. The nearest outcrops were over 150 kilometres away.

The solution he proposed was to move a granite outcrop from Gravenhurst to Toronto. The procedure would cost more than a

The Yorkville rock sparked controversy when it was moved from Gravenhurst to Toronto.

quarter of a million dollars. The first reaction was ridicule and outrage. But the park proceeded. The park opened in 1994 to widespread acclaim from architects and users alike. In one city block, the visitor can travel from a garden with bluebells and trilliums to an alder grove, a wetland, and an herb garden. At the end of the provincial mini-tour, the visitor has lunch or reads a book on top of a billion-year-old rock. And all as the subways rumble below.

The park is on the south side of Cumberland Ave. between Avenue Road and Belair.

Although equally acclaimed, the award-winning Cloud Garden, in the heart of the finance district, has fared less well. In contrast to the much-visited Yorkville Park, Cloud Garden is little more than a haven to the homeless and a gathering place for downtown bike couriers. Sometimes the only "cloud" is marijuana smoke.

Designed by Margaret Priest, the small lot on Temperance Street between Yonge and Bay contains urban woodland, waterfalls, and an observation platform. Situated over the entrance to a park-ing garage is a glass-enclosed "Cloud Forest" conservatory, with its recreation of a tropical rain forest.

Surrounded by the glass towers of the Bay Street brokers, this intriguing urban park won a Governor-General's award for archi-tecture in 1994, and a merit award from the Canadian Society of Landscape Architects the next year. Sadly, it is off the beaten track for downtown shoppers, and ignored by the Bay Street business community. Yet it remains one of Toronto's more unusual parks.

No discussion of Toronto's unusual parks would be complete without the Sculpture Garden. Located on the south side of King St. opposite St. Michael's Cathedral, this tiny parkette was created in 1981 with donations from Louis Odette and the arts advisory board. An oasis in Toronto's congested urban core, it offers artists and sculptors a chance to display their works.

The unusual little Sculpture Garden gives Ontario artists a free venue.

# 13

# The Elevated Wetlands
# of the Don Valley

The elevated wetlands of the Don Valley has drivers on the busy Don Valley Parkway blinking in disbelief. At the Don Mills Road exit are a half dozen massive plant pots. To some passing motorists they look like giant topless tea pots with legs where water cascades from the spout of each into the body of the next. To others, the shapes resemble grotesque mastodons performing some kind of daisy chain.

Their creator is artist Noel Harding, a sculptor who pushes the limits of both sculpture and materials. He is well known for his "Potato Eaters" sculpture. This series of metal structures is 12 to 25 metres in height and each contains a living tree. Harding attracted attention at the Atlanta Olympics as well as at Mississauga City Hall.

Inspired by the work of the Friends of the Don, a group working to restore the natural ecosystem in the much-polluted valley, he deigned the "elevated wetlands." With recycled plastic as a medium for his creation, Harding constructed the containers from polystyrene, a material that keeps out stormy weather, but lets sunlight in.

Even the "soil" itself, except for some top mulch, comes from recycled shredded plastic. In that soil grow a variety of plant species, most of them indigenous to the Don Valley. Water is pumped up from the river to the elephantine planters where the plants leach out

These unusual planters located beside a Toronto expressway
are a natural water purification system.

the toxins before the purified water returns to the river. The plants
are natural water purifiers. Lethbridge and Red Deer are consider-
ing Harding's technique as a way of cleaning their own storm water.

To help fund his labour of love, Harding went to over 70 cor-
porate sources, including the Environment and Plastics Institute of
Canada. After testing smaller prototypes in Lethbridge, he assem-
bled the current creation from giant blocks in a local warehouse.

The six sculptures, which range from eight to 15 metres in
height, are located, three each on either side of the busy Don Valley
Parkway, near Don Mills Road.

Harding's is not the only effort under way to clean up the river.
A short distance downstream, the Friends of the Don managed to
coax $100,000 out of the less-than-environmentally-friendly Ontario
government to excavate a century and a half of industrial residue
from the flood plain. They replaced the landfill with a natural wetland ecosystem, which, like the elevated wetlands, provides free water
purification.

The strange sculptures can be seen close up from the Taylor
Creek Park on Don Mills Road just north of the DVP.

# 14

# Mount Pleasant Cemetery

Nowhere do so many figures from history gather together as in Toronto's Mount Pleasant Cemetery. A simple walk through the grounds leads past the grand mausoleums of the rich and famous. Simple monuments honour those that contributed to the history or disasters or the science of a country. Some are as large as houses, designed by the leading architects of the day. Other monuments are simple stones or plaques. One is shaped like a truck tire.

Mount Pleasant Cemetery is surrounded now by towering apartments, and buffeted by the constant roar of traffic. But when it first opened over a century ago, it was far off in the country.

As York began to burgeon from a few shacks by a swampy harbor into a smoky city called Toronto, it needed a place to bury its dead. At first only those who adhered to the Catholic or Anglican Church were guaranteed a place in which to rest in peace. Then, in 1826, a three-hectare parcel of land on the northwest corner of today's Yonge and Bloor was set aside as a non-denominational graveyard. By 1855, Potter's Field, as it came to be called, contained 6,000 bodies.

But the village of Yorkville to the north and west needed to expand and the cemetery stood in the way. To allow the growth, the remains were exhumed and re-buried in the Necropolis on Winchester Ave. But in less than 20 years, it too was full, and the city fathers needed to look to the country.

A 200-acre farm north of the hamlet of Deer Park (Yonge and St. Clair today) seemed to be the right answer. The grounds were designed by a German-born landscape architect named Henry Engelhardt who drew upon Boston's Mt. Auburn Cemetery for his inspiration. In 1876, when Mount Pleasant cemetery opened, its first interments were some still-unclaimed remains from the old Potter's Field. The elegant landscaped terrain soon became the cemetery of choice for Toronto's wealthiest families and today is a "who's who" of the city's most prominent deceased.

The oldest portion of the cemetery is on Yonge Street with a plaque honouring those Potter's Field remnants. But along with these unnamed poor are the monuments to the rich and famous. Tucked into the side of a gully is the mausoleum of the Simpson family, while above it looms the massive temple-like tomb of the Eatons. Nearby, and easily the most impressive of the mammoth monuments, is that of the Massey family. By 1884, Hart Massey had become the multi-millionaire owner of the Massey-Harris farm implement manufacturing empire. In that year his son, Charles Albert, died of typhoid fever, and six years later his youngest son, Frederick Victor followed, a victim of tuberculosis.

To honour their memory, the elder Massey built Massey Hall, and the Fred Victor Mission respectively. In 1891, he commissioned the Massey mausoleum. Designed by Toronto's leading architect, Edward James Lennox, also famous for old city hall, the King Edward Hotel and Casa Loma, it towers ten metres above the cemetery grounds.

Among the most compelling memorials are there are those to victims of some of Canada's most horrific disasters. The Salvation Army erected a marker to the memory of the 1,477 victims of the ocean liner, the *Empress of Ireland*, which sank in just 15 minutes after colliding with a coal boat in 1914. A monument commissioned by the government of Ontario in 1950 recalls the 119 victims of the *Noronic* that burned while docked at the Toronto waterfront the year before. Yet another honours the 109 victims of Air Canada Flight 621, which crashed and burned while landing at Toronto airport in 1970.

The mausoleum erected by Hart Massey for his two sons
is the tallest in the cemetery.

Many individuals who figured prominently in the history of
the country lie here. Besides politicians and prime ministers are the
graves of Frederick Banting and James Best, co-inventors of insulin;
Alexander Muir, who composed the *Maple Leaf Forever*; and Foster
Hewitt, whose voice remains forever in the memories of Toronto

hockey fans from the 1930s to the 1970s. The strangest monument of all honours Wallace Gordon Chalmers. Inventor of a revolutionary suspension system for trucks, trailers, and wheel chairs, his grave marker is carved out of black granite in the shape of a large radial truck tire.

Anyone wishing to look more closely at the monuments to the rich and famous, can follow the route of the Discovery Walk. The cemetery is part of its ravines walking tour. Or visitors can enjoy the detailed and delightfully anecdotal guide written by Mike Filey.

The grave marker for Wallace Gordon Chambers reflects his passion for motor vehicles.

# Ontario's Most Unusual Buildings

# 15

# Blair's Sheave Tower

The tower stands in the middle of the woods near the historic community of Blair like a miniature mining head frame. This wooden tapering structure that rises four stories above a rushing stream is a rare relic of pioneer Ontario, a sheave tower.

Sheave towers were accessories to gristmills. They used the force of the river to turn a sheave, or a grooved wheel, connected by a pulley to the gristmill. A local mill owner named Allan Bowman built the tower at Blair in 1876 to power a nearby gristmill. The mill, a five-storey structure built in 1849, burned in 1928. Following the fire the power from the sheave tower produced electricity until 1954.

Long a favourite subject for local artists, photographers and historians, it was restored in 1962 by the Waterloo Historical Society. Runoff from nearby subdivisions, however, rushed into the creek, damaged the foundation and put the building's future at risk.

But Blair is one of Ontario's heritage conscious communities. While the owners of the tower worked to clear the sluiceway of silt, the local council in 1986 voted to declare it a heritage structure to save it from demolition.

In 1994, a citizen's group known as Heritage Cambridge used a special revolving fund to buy the crumbling towers. Started in 1984, the revolving fund is a technique ideally suited for cash-strapped

Blair's strange sheave tower resembles a miniature mining headframe.

heritage groups as it allows them to buy a heritage property, and then, using the proceeds from a selling it to a sympathetic buyer, to purchase further properties.

In 1998 Heritage Cambridge sold the tower to the local conservation authority which in turn hired Nicholas Hill, a published sketch artist and one of Ontario's leading heritage architects, to restore the tower. Because much of the wood has rotted it means replacing many planks. For some preservationists, preservation or replication presents a dilemma.

The heritage of Blair goes beyond the sheave tower. The town began life as a milling community on Blair Creek close to the Grand River. Nearby Kitchener and Cambridge present a proximity that dooms historic structures. Yet despite the urban sprawl across the nearby farm fields and the traffic on the 401, the historic integrity of Blair remains. Hotels, homes, mills and cemeteries that date from the early days of settlement have been retained.

But of all the saved and restored historic buildings, the sheave tower remains the most unusual.

# 16

# Kitchener's
## Pioneer Tower

The Kitchener area of Ontario, noted for farmers' markets, Mennonite culture, and rousing Oktoberfest, is also Ontario's unlikely capital of unusual towers. Besides the rustic sheave tower, Kitchener has the stone pioneer tower.

Dominating the Grand River valley from one of its loftiest banks, the tower was built to commemorate Ontario's first inland pioneers. French settlements existed along the Detroit River near Windsor as early as the 1760s. The United Empire Loyalists appeared in the 1780s along the shores of Lakes Ontario and Erie. With the arrival of Joseph Schoerg and Samuel Betzner in 1800 came the vanguard of Ontario's inland pioneers.

By 1805, the German Company had accumulated over 60,000 acres of land along the Grand River. They bought this from the Mohawks who had received it as a reward for their service to the British during the American Revolution. Soon columns of Conestoga wagons were lumbering northward carrying Pennsylvania Dutch and Mennonite settlers. These savvy farmers, with their commitment to farming as not just income but as a divinely ordained way of life, established one of Ontario's most prolific agricultural communities.

The idea for the tower was born more than a century later. To help heal the nationalist wounds caused by the First World War,

This stone tower commemorates the heritage of the German pioneers
in the Waterloo County area.

and to celebrate the German origins of the Waterloo area, William Breithaupt promoted the idea of a memorial tower.

Designed by Toronto Architect, W. A. Langton, the tower was officially opened August 28, 1926. The 22-metre high tower is topped with copper spire of Swiss design, and a weather vane that commemorates the arrival of the colonists in their Conestoga wagons. The body of the tower, made of reinforced concrete, is faced with fieldstones to reflect the hardships in clearing the fields. Visitors enter through a doorway of Indiana limestone and climb to an eight-sided observation deck. Four glazed windows light the stairs. From the deck, the view extends several kilometres up and down the historic river.

Built and owned by the Waterloo County Pioneers Memorial Association, the tower was immediately declared a national historic site by the Historic Sites and Monuments Boards. Then in 1939, concerned over declining maintenance, the Historic Sites Branch took over the tower, and upgraded the grounds, planted grass and built a parking lot.

Farm buildings of the pioneering Betzner and Schoerg families still stand nearby. In the one-half hectare park beside the tower, their family graves are the oldest non-aboriginal inland burial ground in Ontario.

Suburban development has crept closer to the tower and destroyed its rural setting forever. The view over the swirling waters of the Grand River, however, remains unaltered.

The Tower is not staffed and has no admission charge. It lies at the end of Pioneer Tower Road west of King Street near Highway 401 with space for parking. But staff from Parks Canada opens the tower upon request. A phone number is posted on the site.

# 17

# The Ottawa Valley's
# Log Heritage

When pioneers cleared the forests and broke the soil, their first buildings were hurriedly built of log. Shanties managed until a larger second home was built, likewise of log. Once the farmers became established, the owners added their "third" house, usually more substantial and constructed of brick, in areas where clay was abundant, or frame, where timber was more economical.

Throughout most of Ontario, the era of the log building has long passed. In the Ottawa Valley, however, an area rich in logging lore stand barns, houses, and even hotels and schools all made of logs.

On Highway 17, a few minutes drive west of Petawawa, the Ferguson Stopping Place is a complex of a log hotel and barns. It was built in the 1860s to provide rest and refreshment to travelers on the winding Mattawa Road. After being preserved for many years by Atomic Energy of Canada, it is now a private bed and breakfast.

On the grounds of the Waba Cottage Museum, near the hamlet of White Lake, are the relocated log school from Lochwinnoch and a log church from Sand Point. Another log schoolhouse, on its original site, is that on the Opeongo Line, a colonization road that took many early settlers to their first farms. It is now a private home.

Once renowned for its impressive array of log houses and barns, the Opeongo Line has lost much of that heritage to developers who

These log barns, once a pioneer stopping place, are preserved
as a bed and breakfast on Highway 17.

have moved the solid log homes off to chalet developments, or to homeowners who prefer the latest in modern architecture to history. Which makes Davidson's Corners an increasingly valuable heritage site. Long before the Opeongo Line was surveyed, the Davidsons built their first shanty here. They soon built a larger log house, and finally a more comfortable frame dwelling. These, along with the several log barns, still stand and are a singular tribute to the log heritage of the valley, and conscientious owners.

A tour of almost any country road in the Ottawa Valley will reveal a form of barn construction unique to the area, the "string" barns. In a land where farmers often could not afford to replace their original log barns with newer structures, they simply added another barn to the end of the first. Some of these barns kept on "growing" until a "string" of them, sometimes as many as six, encased the farm yard.

But log buildings are found not only in the countryside. A few of the valley villages also sport many log buildings right in town. The hamlet of Ashton, just south of Highway 7 and east of Carleton Place has log buildings. Burnstown on the Madawaska River has log structures as well.

Even Ottawa itself hides an interesting vestige of this unique era. Tucked away on Guigues Street, four blocks north of the popular Byward Market, and surrounded by newer houses and apartments, sits a log house, a reminder of the days when Ottawa was a remote mill town named simply Bytown.

The legacy in log is a link with a pioneer past not duplicated anywhere else in Ontario.

A log church and school reflect the remarkable log heritage of the Ottawa Valley area.

# 18

# Castle Kilbride:
## A Countryside Palace

Not many buildings in Ontario warrant the name "castle." But castle best describes a magnificent mansion found on the main street of the little village of Baden.

Like most 19th century mansions, Castle Kilbride is a monument to the excesses of the industrial age. While lacking the romance of the railways or the gold rushes that brought so much wealth to so many, the production of linseed oil made James Livingston wealthy beyond his dreams.

Born to a Scottish weaver, Livingston arrived in Canada in 1854 at the age of 16 where he worked first on a farm, then in a flax mill. In 1864, along with his brother, he rented a flax mill in the Waterloo County mill town of Wellesley. Within just three years the pair built their own flax mill in Baden, adding a linseed oil mill to their operation. Linseed oil is made by pressing flaxseed and is a key ingredient in paint and soap.

By 1877, Livingston was known as the "Flax and Oil King of Canada." And every king needs his castle. Livingston built a massive Italianate mansion in his new hometown. Set back from the road, and surrounded by a wrought iron fence and elegant garden, its tall slender cupola became a landmark for miles around. The mansion was a palatial home for Livingston, his wife Louise and their 11 children. The castle remained in the family until 1949. In

Castle Kilbride is a Baden landmark.

1988 it was sold to a private developer, and the contents auctioned off. For five years the building sat empty, deteriorating, its elegance slipping away.

But, as so often happens in small communities, the local residents were not about to let their most prominent building disappear. In 1993, the Township of Wilmot bought the property and began the work of restoration. The building contains a wonderful array of period furnishings. But the uncovering of the original interior decorating sets this mansion apart. Mouldings and murals cover the ceilings. Remarkable examples of "trompe d'oeil" paintings dominate the main hall. This painting technique, which uses brush techniques to create a feeling of depth, makes the columns, statues, and vases of the hallway seem real. This artwork combined with the architecture prompted the federal government to declare the Castle a National Historic Site.

Castle Kilbride, which also contains the Wilmot municipal offices, is open from 1:00 - 4:00, Tuesdays through Sundays. A small admission fee is charged.

# 19

# Her Majesty's Royal Chapel of the Mohawks

One of the least known stories in the history of Ontario links Royalty with Ontario's First Nations. During both the American colonial rebellion, and the War of 1812, the Mohawks provided invaluable help to the British. Their knowledge of the land, and their warfare techniques often brought victory where traditional British strategies would have meant defeat. As a result, the Mohawks were rewarded with extensive grants of land.

A wonderful stone church is located in the First Nations territory of Tyendinaga just east of Belleville. Built in 1843, it is one of just six Royal chapels built outside England and one of only two in Ontario. The other is the better-known St. Paul's Royal Chapel near Brantford. While Ontario's oldest Protestant church, the Brantford chapel built in 1785 is famous, the little church at Tyendinaga has been largely ignored.

Yet the story of the Tyendinaga chapel goes back far beyond the American rebellion, to the year 1710, when four chiefs of the Iroquois Confederacy visited England. Treated like visiting royalty, they met with Queen Anne to request both military aid and missionaries. In response, Queen Anne ordered the construction of a Royal chapel at Johnstown in New York state. When the building was finished in 1711, the Queen sealed the relationship with gifts of a double silver communion set and a reed organ. Furthermore, she commanded

Few know of the forgotten Royal Chapel at Deseronto.

that portraits of the four chiefs be painted, and hung in Kensington Palace, London.

With the defeat of the British in 1783, the Mohawks could no longer remain in New York. They were given grants of land along the Grand River and on the shores of the Bay of Quinte. Royal chapels were built in each location.

The Tyendinaga chapel contains several historic treasures. Here are a triptych in the Mohawk language, a bell given by King George III, a royal coat of arms given by King George V, a Bible from Queen Victoria, and a communion chalice from the present monarch, Queen Elizabeth II. But the most historic of its treasurers is the beautiful Communion Silver given by Queen Anne herself in 1711.

The chapel also commemorates one its most celebrated native sons, Dr. Oronhyateka. The first accredited native doctor in North America, Dr. Oronhyateka was a member of Canada's first Wimbledon Rifle Team, a founder of the Independent Order of Foresters, and a personal friend of the Prince of Wales. He died in 1907 and is buried at the Royal Chapel, commemorated with a plaque and a window he donated.

A national historic site, the beautiful stone church is being restored with $850,000 from Heritage Canada, church members, and individual and personal donations. The church commands a rise of land about 4 kilometres north west of the town of Deseronto. Directional indicators lead the way from Highway 49.

# 20

# Emo's Unusual Norlund Chapel

Many churches have lost their steeples, sometimes to fire, sometimes to aging. But the Norlund chapel in Emo Ontario is a steeple that has lost its church.

Emo is in the far northwestern reaches of Ontario. The land is flat and the soil is black and almost treeless. Geologically, this part of Ontario is an extension of the prairies. To reach this rich land, the first settlers travelled along the wide Rainy River by steamer. Along the way villages grew up at the many little steamer landings. In 1904, the railway arrived, eliminating many of the steamer villages.

Midway between the railway towns of Fort Francis and Rainy River, Emo got a station and became a busy town. Thanks to its origins as a steamer stop, main street developed along the riverfront.

As it grew, Emo attracted businesses, schools and churches. In 1935, St. Patrick's Roman Catholic Church was built on the outskirts of the village. Its twenty-foot high wooden steeple was topped with a six-foot high wrought iron cross.

In 1971, lightning struck and destroyed the church. Incredibly, the steeple survived nearly unscathed. To celebrate the miracle, Elmer Norlund and Ed Sletmoen designed a chapel around the steeple. Its size, just two metres by three, is barely enough to allow eight people to fill the building. Now non-denominational, it is open to worshipers of all faiths. The Emo steeple is one of the world's smallest churches.

The churchless steeple is North America's smallest chapel.

# Amazing
# Monuments

# 21

# The Cryptic Gravestone
## of Rushes Cemetery

Visitors to the Rushes Cemetery west of Waterloo could only scratch their heads in puzzlement at the mass of letters that covers the strange grave marker. While the size of the stone, and the graphic etched onto it are not unlike those found on thousands of other 19th century grave markers, the message definitely is not. For covering the entire face of the gravestone is a mass of 225 letters and numbers, with no apparent order or sense. Yet, the message is in there. If you can figure it out.

Rushes cemetery is an ordinary looking pioneer cemetery. Atop a hill, the cemetery is neatly trimmed and surrounded by peaceful farmland. Cars rush past on the busy road. An occasional Mennonite buggy creaks by at a more leisurely pace. Nearby stand the attractive rural villages of Wellesley and Crosshill. Fading grave markers list the deaths of many early pioneers in the area.

In the far corner of Rushes cemetery stands the now famous "Bean" marker.

Samuel Bean was born in 1842 in Wilmot Township, and became an Evangelical minister as well as a medical doctor. Local legend claims he read the entire Bible no less than 65 times. In 1865 he married Henrietta Furry who died only seven months later. His second marriage, to Susanna Clegg, didn't last much longer. To commemorate their passing he devised what may be one of Ontario's

Can you solve the message on this odd grave marker?

most mystifying and most visited grave markers. Where his two first wives lay buried, he encrypted a message in what at first glance is a nonsensical and random arrangement of letters that totally covers the front of the marker.

While the dedication may appear impossible to decipher, by determining where to start the message and the order in which the words are spelled, the message is suddenly and plainly revealed.

The original grave marker deteriorated to the point where the letters were unreadable. But to help keep alive this interesting piece of local history, heritage proponents in 1982 erected a duplicate stone beside the original.

Bean's third marriage lasted longer. Bean himself, who died in 1904, lies buried by his third wife in the Strasburg, Ontario, cemetery.

The grave marker itself is illustrated here, and we invite the reader to try and solve the puzzle. Clue: Don't start at either the top or the bottom. Rather, begin at the seventh column from the left, and at the seventh letter from the top. The answer is at the back of this book.

Rushes cemetery is located three kilometres north of the attractive country village of Wellesley on Waterloo Regional Road 5.

# 22

# The Tragedy of Jumbo

Looming on the hill on the west side of St. Thomas is the silhouette of a huge elephant. This is the remarkable statue of Jumbo, the largest elephant ever held in captivity. At St. Thomas the best known of all circus animals met his untimely demise.

The circus had just ended its evening show on September 15, 1885. Jumbo and his midget friend, Tom Thumb, were returning along the track to the circus train when they were surprised by the sudden appearance of an unscheduled freight train. Jumbo was hit and thrown forward into a line of cars on a siding. A tusk was driven into his brain and he died shortly after.

Captured when young, Jumbo lived three years in the Paris zoo. He was then traded to the London zoo for a rhinoceros. There he grew into one of the largest elephants known to experts. But he also adopted himself to his human captors with his gentle ways.

This "gentle giant" came to the attention of American circus promoter P.T. Barnum. In 1881, ignoring furious protests, including one directly from Queen Victoria, he bought Jumbo from the London zoo for $10,000, a huge sum at the time. Court actions were launched to prevent the sale. But Barnum was unmoved.

Jumbo's departure from London was heart-rending. When he realized he was being moved, he lay down on the street in resistance, as the wailing of a female elephant filled the air.

A life-sized statue commemorates the famous circus elephant.

Once in North America, the huge elephant became an even greater hit than Barnum could have dreamed, filling the streets, and, more important, the tents. But that all ended in St. Thomas.

After Jumbo's death, Barnum displayed the ghoulish hide for another two years before donating it to the Tufts University in Boston. It remained there until 1975 when it was destroyed in a fire.

To commemorate the hundredth anniversary of Jumbo's death in l985, the St. Thomas Jumbo Foundation commissioned a statue. Designed and constructed by Winston Bronnum of New Brunswick, the life-sized statue is made of reinforced concrete and weighs thirty-eight tons. Fittingly it was shipped not by train, but by two trucks along the Trans Canada Highway. The statue drew as much attention as Jumbo did in real life a hundred years earlier.

# 23

# Monument to Murder:
## the Reesor Massacre

Traveling the northern Trans Canada Highway through Ontario is an unusual experience. The highway itself is a newcomer to the landscape. Once a land of railway towns, where stores and houses huddled beside a little railway station, the highway now dominates.

Even so, the car still seems a stranger to this area. Passing through the one-time railway villages, then into the countryside where most farms have failed, and then through the bushland, before emerging into the next farm clearings, and the next little town. It comes as a surprise to see above an overgrown field a monument to a murder.

This is the Great Clay Belt. After the First World War plans to colonize the area failed when the ex-soldiers and city-dwellers recoiled at the harsh conditions and returned south. During this flight, many of the railway towns failed. Reesor Siding was one of them. The only industry was logging at the Spruce Falls pulp mill in Kapuskasing or in the bush camps.

In January 1963, more than 1,000 members of the United Brotherhood of Carpenters and Joiners working in eight bush camps staged a wildcat strike to protest the slow progress of contract talks. Independent non-union loggers, angry at losing money, and unable to feed their families, opposed the strike. They formed an

This Northern Ontario monument recalls a tragic labour dispute.

80-car cavalcade to express their frustration. Four days later the union countered with a cavalcade of more than 290 cars.

Tensions ran high. The company refused to negotiate until the workers returned to the camps. The workers refused to return until the company began to negotiate. Calls for the provincial government to name a conciliator went unheeded. The government likely worsened the situation by granting permits to independent loggers. Most of the logs were brought out to flat cars at Reesor Siding for shipment once the strike ended.

Faced with an injunction that would prevent them from picketing the mill, the strikers decided to picket at Reesor Siding. On the night of February 11, they arrived at Reesor Siding. Twenty armed loggers were waiting for them. Shots rang out in the cold night air and three strikers fell dead. Another nine lay wounded. The worst labour violence in the area devastated the entire community.

Nineteen loggers were brought to trial. Without proof of who fired the guns, they were acquitted. The stark monument, which rises incongruously above the flat landscape of the deserted siding, speaks for itself. In a fitting act of justice, the workers now own the mill.

# 24

# The Forgotten
## Tecumseh Monument

Sometimes monuments are in unusual locations. The Reesor Monument and the Dyer Memorial in the woods near Huntsville are examples. Monuments to the war dead are deservedly prominently located. The well-known Isaac Brock monument towers above the crest of the Niagara Escarpment at Queenston near the spot where he was slain during the War of 1812.

But a little known monument to a Shawnee chief named Tecumseh goes unheralded. His monument sits inconspicuously surrounded by the litter of a roadside picnic ground on a secondary highway near a little-known town, He was a great leader and a Canadian war hero that is all but forgotten.

This modest bronze plaque commemorates
the unsung Canadian war hero Tecumseh.

Tecumseh was one of Canada's unsung war heroes who turned back the American invasion of 1812.

Tecumseh was born in 1768 near the Ohio Valley. Settlers were streaming west from the former thirteen colonies on the coast. Although the Americans had promised the various tribes that all the land north of the Ohio River would be theirs, pressure from would-be settlers, and anti-Indian sentiment, quickly rendered the promise worthless. To counter the advancing frontier, Tecumseh and his brother, the Prophet, tried to rally the tribes to stand firm.

With the war of 1812 Tecumseh found an ally in the British. In exchange for a commitment to honour the promise of land that the Americans had made, he agreed to help the British. Tecumseh was as good as his word and was key to British victory at Fort Detroit. Following a disastrous naval defeat on Lake Erie in 1813, the British retreated up the valley of the Thames. On October 5th, the pursuing Americans routed them at the Battle of Moraviantown. As the

British fled in disarray, Tecumseh stayed to fight. Sensing his own death, he handed his sword to a comrade, asking that it be given to his son. Moments later, the chief was killed.

Without his inspiration, the tribes south of the border gave up their resistance to the incursions of the settlers. While the British eventually repelled the Americans in their attempts to invade Canada, they made no land gains of their own. The Ohio Valley was lost to the Indians for good.

To honour the chief, and the place where he fell, the National Historic Sites and Monuments placed a bronze mould of the fallen hero, along with a native petroglyph carved into six blocks of stone. Next to it a plaque placed by the citizens of Thamesville commemorates the battle and the chief.

The monument is in a picnic area beside Highway 2, about 3 kilometres east of Thamesville.

# 25

# The Canadian
## Warplane Museum

The unusual aircraft noise from Mount Hope International Airport near Hamilton is likely to be a vintage Hawker Hurricane or Avro Lancaster bomber.

One of Ontario's most unusual and most exciting museums is the Canadian Warplane Heritage Museum. Displayed in a brand new 103,000 square foot building are 35 vintage aircraft, 21 of them in flying condition. They range from the ancient Boeing Stearman bi-plane to a CF-86 Sabre jet.

The brainchild of Dennis Bradley, Allan Ness, John Weir, and Tim Matthews, the warplane museum began with the acquisition of a single Fairey Firefly. As the collection grew, the aircraft gradually took over a pair of World War Two hangars at the aging airport. In the 1980s the airport was upgraded in anticipation of increasing international flights.

As the dreams of an international airport dwindled, the vision of a new warplane museum grew. In 1993 a fire destroyed five aircraft in one of the hangars. The museum pushed for a new facility. In 1996, with funding from the Canada Infrastructure Works program, the state-of-the-art museum was ready. In April it was officially opened by the museum's patron, Prince Charles.

This unique display allows today's generation an opportunity for a first-hand look at the war in the air. And to make it even more

Canada's warplane museum contains several working historic aircraft.

real, visitors may ride in the Stearman bi-plane, or a Harvard trainer.

The museum also contains a library with 4000 volumes on aviation history and archives with more than 2,000 photos.

The museum is on Airport Road east of Fiddlers Green Road south of the City of Hamilton.

# Hidden Valleys

# 26

# The Sudden Splendour of the Elora Gorge

Suddenly and unexpectedly in the flat farmlands northwest of Guelph, there appears a crack. No ordinary crack, the Elora Gorge is a canyon two kilometres long and more than 20 metres deep, a wonderland of hanging gardens, caves, caverns, dry valleys, and odd looking rock formations.

The gorge represents the outcropping of a dolostone formation known by geologists as the Guelph Formation. Unusually rich in fossils and reefs, this 400 million year old rock emerges at the surface here. When the glaciers left the area about 20,000 years ago, the waters began to wear down the rock until a long gorge took shape. The remnant of that post-glacial torrent is today's Grand River.

The various shapes and formations found in the gorge have fanciful names. Dividing the waters of a foaming waterfall, the *Tooth of Time* is formed by the triangular remains of an eroded ledge. Close by, the *Lovers Leap* promontory juts into the fork formed by Irwin Creek and the Grand River. Further downstream, *the Castles* were etched by the waters of a long vanished river that plunged over the edge of the cliff, leaving a series of rock columns that resemble castle ramparts. An extinct waterfall carved out a 40-metre wide amphitheatre known as the *Punch Bowl*.

The *Cascade* is a filmy plunge of a small creek into the gully. Across from it the *Hanging Garden* shows off various mosses and

This unexpected crack in flat farmland contains many unusual rock formations.

ferns drooping from an overhanging cliff. Several caves along the riverbank make unusual swimming holes, and the *Hole in the Rock* provides passage for a trail right through the rock itself.

The strange beauty and the appeal of the rushing river have turned the gorge into a popular park. Trails follow both riverbanks, and wind along the bottom of the gorge. Inner tubes are rented to those who wish to cool off in a hot summer day by floating downstream. The river here has no waterfalls or rapids. Those who prefer to remain dry can enjoy the gorge from the trail, from viewpoints at Lovers Leap, or from the mill in Elora.

The Elora Gorge Conservation Area is a short distance west of the attractive village of Elora.

# 27

# The Rock Glen Gorge

While no one is going to find any dinosaur bones in the Rock Glen gorge, they will find hundreds of equally ancient creatures.

Located in the Rock Glen Conservation Area, the gorge was created by the relentless erosion of the Ausable River into ancient layers of limestone and shale. As the ancestors of today's shellfish died, they drifted to the ocean bottom where they hardened into layers of bedrock. Above them, more layers were deposited, and they also hardened. When the last glaciers finally melted, the waters of today's Ausable River eroded into the soil and then the bedrock to gradually expose the former seabeds.

Fossils appear in much of Ontario's bedrock. Rock hard fossils require a pick to remove. But what makes the fossils in the damp little valley so unusual is that during rainfalls the clay turns soft and the rocky shells can be removed by hand.

The most common fossils are the branch-shaped stag horn coral or plant-like crinoids. Less common are the snail-like trilobites. The most interesting are the butterfly-shaped brachiopods, which the Chinese call "stone butterflies."

While the fossils can be found everywhere, the footing is tricky. The hunting grounds lie deep in the 25-metre chasm where the stream trickles around boulders. Yet the best time to fossil hunt is after a rainstorm, when the runoff washes more fossils out of the mud.

Fossil hunters can dig the ancient critters right out of the mud.

Rock Glen Conservation Authority has a few rules. Picks and shovels are not permitted, nor is collecting from the valley walls themselves. Loose specimens are everywhere. The park has a museum and staff with helpful brochures.

The 25-hectare Conservation Area is on County Road 12, close to the village of Arkona.

# 28

# St. David's Buried Gorge

More than 23,000 years ago, the mighty Niagara River plunged through a narrow gorge nearly a kilometre from where it flows today. Today that gorge is all but invisible. But those who visit the Falls, once they finish with the thundering cataract and the whirlpool, and yes, the casino, might go back in time to where mighty Niagara once roared. While locals call it the Whirlpool Golf Course, geologists name it the St. Davids Buried Gorge.

At that time, a pre-glacial Niagara River rushed down what is known today as the Whirlpool Gorge. But instead of making a sharp

A plaque commemorates the former railway across the buried gorge.

right-angle bend, as it does now, it went straight ahead, through the current site of the whirlpool, through the Niagara Escarpment and on to a smaller Lake Ontario.

Then the glaciers arrived and filled the gorge with debris. After melting back to the brink of the Niagara Escarpment, the ice mass rested as a lake formed in front of it on top of the Escarpment. The glaciers continued their retreat northward, away from the cuesta, and the waters of the lake drained over the lip.

One of those drainage points was near Queenston, where the river passes the Escarpment today. For ten thousand years the river wore back the rocks carving a new chasm until it reached the earlier gorge. The point at which it broke through the wall and into the older canyon is marked today by the odd-looking sharp turn that the river makes at the whirlpool. The river then took another nine thousand years to erode back to the brink over which it plunges today.

The pre-historic gorge was once a major rattlesnake nesting area.

The buried gorge today remains a deep canyon carved into the Escarpment. But it is filled with glacial sands and gravels, and no one can see it. It extends 3.2 kilometres from the whirlpool to St. Davids and is ¼ kilometre wide, and more than 80 metres deep.

The settlers called it the Bowman Creek ravine and knew it as a haven for timber rattlesnakes. Now thought to be extinct, the large snakes migrated down the gorge, by the thousands, to winter at its base before retreating back up to the heights for the summer. The reptiles were as unpopular with the early native inhabitants as they were with the settlers. While the Indians set fire to their hibernation site, the settlers turned their hogs loose into the area. One snake kill was reported to have netted more than 500 serpents. The last reliable reporting of a timber rattler occurred in 1959.

In 1893, the Niagara Falls Park and River Railway built a trestle across the ravine, before filling it in twenty years later. Now part of a walking trail along the gorge, the buried trestle is identified by a cut stone marker. Parts of it poke through the manicured lawns. From this marker it is possible to see clearly the large size of this buried gorge. Although filled in beside the road, it cuts a wide swath to the whirlpool more than a half kilometre away. Hikers can follow a long flight of steps into the gully, and on to the shores of the river.

At the north end, the gully breaks through the Escapement near the village of St. David where St. Paul Ave. traces the depression formed by the buried gorge. While Niagara offers much to see, sometimes what can't be seen is as interesting and unusual.

# 29

# White River's
## Strange Grand Canyon

In 1972, rain poured *sans cess* upon the little town of Sainte-Jean Vianney Quebec, just across the Saguenay River from Jonquiere. A bus suddenly swerved. Before it lay a gaping pit where the road had been. Somewhere in the morass lay the village, and more than 30 victims.

The phenomenon known as land slippage occurs when sub-surface layers of silt and clay become so saturated that they turn into a soup-like liquid and slip away. The result is a canyon where none had existed before. The slippage at St. Jean Vianney was nearly one kilometre across and one and half kilometres long. The disaster made headlines around the world. In eastern Ontario, the village of Lemieux, located on the same kind of soil, was evacuated before disaster could strike. A few years later, the press reported a huge landslide tore away a vast area of riverbank just east of the abandoned townsite.

But when these landslips occur in remote woodland in northern Ontario, no one hears of the unchallenged powers of nature.

Twenty-five kilometres east of the town of Marathon, a dirt road leads past Rouse Lake to a gaping canyon 1 kilometre long, ⅓ kilometre wide, and 50 metres deep.

Like the land slippage near Jonquiere, it unleashed a torrent of

Created by land slippage, this canyon is a natural work in progress.

mud that MNR officials liken to "ten tandem trucks hauling ten loads a day for twenty years."

The land is always on the verge of moving. This expanding canyon has engulfed two roads and large chunk of forest. From the sounds of water running beneath the ground more slippage will occur.

# 30

# Algonquin Park's Incredible Barren Canyon

At first glance it is hard to believe that Ontario has a canyon so deep and so precipitous. While the magnificent Ouimet Canyon of northern Ontario is longer and wider, and displays a collection of rare Arctic plants, the canyon on the Barren River in northeastern Algonquin Park is both narrower and considerably deeper.

The origins are as unique as the canyon itself. After the rocks of the Canadian Shield formed billions of years ago, they lay buried beneath the deposits of an ancient sea. Under the weight of that sea, the sandy deposits gradually hardened into limestone. When the entire area heaved upward, the limestone cap fragmented into fault lines that ran in a northwest to southeast direction.

Millions of centuries later, as the great ice sheets that covered Ontario retreated northward, the melt waters drained along the fault lines. One channel became the outlet for an enormous post-glacial lake named Lake Algonquin. Some geologists estimate the torrent equaled a thousand Niagaras. As the ice sheet continued its northerly retreat the meltwaters found a lower outlet that became the Mattawa and Ottawa Rivers.

Since then, erosion has continued sculpting magic on the canyon. The harsh freeze and thaw action of the frigid Algonquin winters cause chunks of rock to cascade into the valley far below.

For a few decades the Barren River echoed to the shouts of

loggers pushing the logs downstream to mills at Petawawa and Pembroke. After the last drive ended in 1930, the cleft became an awe-inspiring destination for canoeists and hikers. Birdwatchers observe such unlikely species as the swamp-loving Yellow-bellied Flycatcher and the Common Yellowthroat along the cliffs, as well as the rare Bald Eagle.

The dizzying Barren River canyon is the most spectacular chasm in Ontario.

Thanks to Algonquin's park planners the canyon is easy to visit and photograph. From the parking area 11 kilometres west of the Sand Lake gate, a 1.5 kilometre loop trail leads to the lip of the precipice, a dizzying 100 metres above the river below. The trail is occasionally steep, and the edge unfenced. From the top, breathtaking views extend far downstream to the east.

Canoes can launch at a number of landings. The portion of the river between the soaring walls is relatively placid, and makes for a pleasant afternoon to view one of Ontario's more unusual and spectacular geological wonders.

Hikers must use caution as the gorge is unfenced.

# Nature's Puzzles

# 31

# The Hell Holes

A walk through the forest can sometimes be a dangerous thing, not necessarily from wolves or bears or deer hunters, but from a careless step into a hole, especially when the hole leads to Hell.

The limestone ridge along the Salmon River north of Napanee contains some of the area's most unusual natural features. There are caves, crevices, canyons and odd looking columns, but the strangest of its oddities are what locals call the "hell holes."

To early settlers, unfamiliar with geological freaks of nature, these holes in the forest floor seemed to have no end. While most were no bigger than a foxhole, a few were large enough to allow a human to squeeze through. Those who braved the descent found caverns went endlessly in all different directions. The Devil's Horse Stable was said to extend over several hundred metres.

But those who are familiar with geological phenomenon call them "karst" features. Karst topography occurs when limestone layers beneath a hard upper layer dissolve in water. This weathering causes caves and caverns, and the hell holes. Similar to caves, the holes in the forest floor can open into large pitch-black rooms, some large enough to hold twenty people.

While there are other locations in Ontario, the ridge by Salmon River in the vicinity of Roblindale offers the greatest concentration of these cavities.

Early pioneers thought that these bottomless pits led straight to Hell.

There are two easy ways to locate them. The Ontario Field Naturalists Guide describes access along the CPR tracks that lead east from Highway 41, immediately south of Roblindale. Walk northeast along the railway for about 1.5 kilometres to the milepost 67 marker. Turn south and follow any of the ridges and gorges until you are the edge of the deepest gully.

But perhaps a simpler way would be to drive to the privately run Hell Holes Park. This 100-hectare site contains a self-guided trail, 3.2 kilometres long, that follows the ridge. Visitors will find natural rock bridges, eerie canyons lined with layered cliffs and columns, and a hellhole large enough to enter. The owners have installed a ladder to permit easy descent. Flashlights are necessary and can by rented at the park office. The park, with playground, snack bar, and picnic facilities, lies a short distance north of Centreville Road east from Highway 41.

# 32

# Temagami's Tall Pines

The stately white pine, Ontario's provincial tree, is threatened with extinction. Even through Ontario's natural resources ministry purports to honour the white pine tree as a symbol of Ontario's natural heritage, that agency, along with their partners in the logging industry, have done their utmost to hasten its elimination. The few remaining stands are even more of a treasure. Temagami in northern Ontario has the best trees.

Throughout the 19th century and into the 20th, loggers removed entire swaths of the tall pines. What the loggers didn't take, fires fueled by their refuse did. Today, replanting and timber management plans are in effect for Crown lands. Unfortunately, neither is adhered to. Ontario's forests continue to disappear at an alarming rate.

The area around Temagami, situated about a two-hour's drive from North Bay, is a relic wilderness. Lakes and rivers seem surrounded by tall pine forests. ("Seem" because the practice of the logging companies is to remain back from the shorelines so that their activities are not visible). Of Temagami's tall pine areas, the Lady Evelyn Smoothwater Park, accessible only by canoe, is the best known. The ministry plans to turn parts of the forest over to the loggers.

A less-known tall pine area is available to those who travel by car and foot. Located immediately east of the village of Temagami,

The White Bear tall pine forest at Temagami.

stands the White Bear Forest, named after a local First Nations family. Despite its proximity to roads, railways, and loggers, the area has never been logged, mined or otherwise disturbed.

Walking trails wind through the forest, and range from one to two and a half-hours in duration. For those wishing to linger, a few wilderness campsites are located along them. While many ecological features dot the route, from red pine stands to beaver meadows, the highlight is the grove of soaring white pines on the north shore of Pleasant Lake. The tall trees are found in several other locations throughout the forest. The forest also offers scenic lookouts. Caribou Mountain overlooks the village of Temagami and the lakes and woods around it.

The best access to the White Bear Forest is from the parking area in Finlayson Point Park on Highway 11.

The village of Temagami offers small restaurants, motels, and the attractive little stone ONR railway station, now being restored by a local heritage trust.

# 33

# The Strange Story
## of Crawford Lake

The Crawford Lake Conservation Area is a rare find. Like many others, it sits atop the Niagara Escarpment, with wonderful views, and trails through a tall hardwood forest. And like many others, it has a small lake. But this lake makes no waves.

Geologists have a special name for it. The call it a "meromictic" lake, which means that, relative to its surface area, it is proportionately deeper than most lakes. This results in many unusual lake effects. The upper portion of the lake seldom mixes with the lower portion. This is like two lakes, one on top of the other. The lower levels are deprived of oxygen, which would normally come from the air above. Lack of oxygen leads to a remarkably good state of preservation of the materials on the bottom.

Such preservation allows scientists to read the debris. They can determine with much more certainty what the area around it was like thousands, or even tens of thousands of years ago. Lake Crawford is estimated to be at least 15,000 years old.

Among the layers of silt that cover the bottom, scientists uncovered evidence of pre-historic Huron habitation. The discovery sent archaeologists searching. Near the lake they uncovered the remains of a major Huron village. Previously unknown, the village contained nine long houses and a population of about 450. The village dates from around 1430. Numerous other village sites

Crawford Lake is one of only two deep oxygen-deprived meromictic lakes in Ontario.

were subsequently recorded in the surrounding hills and valleys.

Not only is the shape and morphology of the lake unusual, so too is its origin. Unlike other lakes, which form along existing rivers or in low lands, this one happened, some theorize, when a cave beneath the upper limestone layer suddenly collapsed. Water rushed in from underground streams, quickly filling the cavity. Another theory suggests the lake fills an ancient post-glacial spillway. Because the lake is so deep relative to its width, there is little wave action on its surface. There are only two such "waveless" lakes in Ontario, the other being in Algonquin Park.

Following the departure of the Hurons, Murray Crawford operated a sawmill on its shores before adopting the site as a summer retreat for his family. In 1969 the land was sold to the Halton Region

Conservation Authority who laid out trails to the lake, and recreated the Huron village, complete with palisade. So authentic is the habitation, and the depiction of the lifestyles of its inhabitants, that the village has become a must for many school children from across Ontario.

A 1.4-kilometre path leads to the lake where interpretive stations explain its unusual origins and composition. A 7.2-kilometre trail leads further afield, through the dark woodlands, leading to a lookout point over the scenic Nassagaweya Canyon, and Rattlesnake Point beyond. The Crawford Lake Conservation Area is on Guelph Line a short distance south of Highway 401.

# 34

# Ontario's Southern Prairie

To find a touch of Canada's prairie landscape in northwestern Ontario might be expected. But to find it in southern Ontario near Windsor is a surprise.

The idea that southern Ontario once exhibited a "prairie" landscape is puzzling. Most believe that pre-historic Ontario consisted of dense dark forests broken only by small native clearings. But prairies? Not only were they widespread, but one of the largest remnants is right inside the city of Windsor.

Before the European settlers marched across Ontario, axe in hand, Ontario's forests were more than 750 square kilometres of tall grass prairie and oak savanna. Of this, nearly two-thirds was located within today's Essex, Kent and Lambton counties. Smaller prairie landscapes occurred in Elgin County, Brantford, near Lake Simcoe and Rice Lake, and even within the Greater Toronto Area.

Typically, the tallgrass prairies consisted of blue stem grass up to three metres high, prairie cord grass and Indian grass, while here and there in the meadows stood oak trees.

Open landscape was irresistible to settlers. The stoneless soils were soon cultivated.

An accident of history spared the prairie remnant in Windsor. Prior to the arrival of the British, the French settled much of the Windsor area. Because the Detroit River was their first means of

Tall grasses dominate one of Ontario's unusual prairie landscapes.

transportation, they lived close together along the waterfront. Their farms were divided into long thin strips of property. Because the rear portions were so far from the river the prairie on them was idle and unaltered. Though industrial and residential development was proposed for the area, wars and depressions intervened. By the 1950s these prairie back lands remained in a largely natural state.

In 1971, recognizing this landscape represented the last one per cent of Ontario's ancient prairies, the Department of Lands and Forests and the Quetico Foundation and the Nature Conservancy of

Ontario purchased the properties to manage and preserve this nearly vanished natural legacy. Now, safely within the Ojibway Prairie Provincial Nature Reserve, this 91-hectare remnant is managed carefully. Because one of the natural forces in the creation of prairies is fire, management practice includes controlled burns in the spring. Flowering plants and the tall grasses are in full bloom by August.

The Reserve also forms part of a larger area known as the Ojibway Prairie Remnants Area, a 360-hectare complex of smaller prairie remnants, partly managed by the City of Windsor.

While the provincial reserve lies along the south side of the Titcombe Road allowance, Windsor's Tallgrass Prairie Heritage Park sits to the north. A small parking area is accessible from Matchette Road in the west end of Windsor. The Ojibway Nature Centre, also on Matchette Road, offers an interpretative program.

# 35

# Houghton's Sand Hills

Towering more than 120 metres above the waters of Lake Erie, Ontario's biggest sandbox, the Houghton Sand Hills are higher than the Scarborough Bluffs.

As the glaciers of the last great ice age melted northward, a huge lake, four times the size of Lake Erie formed along the edge of the icy lobe. As the torrents of melt water raced into the lake a huge delta took shape. The glaciers melted back still further, allowing the great lake to drain away, leaving today's Lake Erie, and a monster pile of sand. The winds began to blow across the treeless wasteland. The sand piled into huge dunes that towered above the lake.

Thousands of years later, as settlers took up land in the nearby forests, the geological phenomenon did not go unnoticed. In 1877 the Atlas of Norfolk County, normally a conservative and understated tome, gushed uncharacteristically that there was "nothing more astonishing than the immense mounds of pure sand, standing upon the edge of the precipitous cliffs which border the lake."

One of the first to take advantage of the heights was the United States Lake Survey which placed a 70-foot observatory on the summit. A similar tower on Long Point and a third across the lake in Pennsylvania helped map the navigation charts used by sailors to this day.

The sand hills attracted curiosity seekers as well. In the 1890s,

Ontario's biggest "sandbox" towers 120 metres above Lake Erie.

George Alton the owner, charged 10 cents a visit. A geological oddity became a tourist attraction.

The hills came perilously close to extinction in the early 1900s when a glass manufacturer tried to purchase the sand for export to the United States. Alton resisted and the sand pile was saved. In 1958, a campground was opened. Constant improvements to the unusual grounds have made it one of the more popular privately owned tourist attractions on Lake Erie.

From the roadside, the hills look like an uninspiring grassy mound. A short walk to the top reveals their dizzying height above the lake below. Pure sand from crest to beach, the bluff hills displays ever-changing layers and shapes. For the kids, the hills are a huge sandbox, where they can tumble down the gentler slopes, or built endless castles.

Sand Hill Park is located 12 kilometres west of Port Burwell on Regional Road 42.

A pre-historic river deposited this soaring sand bluff on Lake Erie.

# 36

# The Torrance Barrens

In the middle of the idyllic Muskoka Lakes country, known throughout North America for their classical Canadian beauty, lies an oddly barren and desolate landscape. So eerie and unusual is this landscape that Canadian film director, David Cronenberg, master of the horror movie genre, chose the area as the location for his bizarre film, *Naked Lunch*.

The Muskoka Lakes, one of Canada's premier recreational playgrounds, lie in the ancient granite heart of the Canadian Shield. Sparkling lakes nestled amid the pine-laden outcrops inspire artists and photographers. The desolation found in the Torrance Barrens seems dramatically out of place.

The Barrens are located south of the village of Torrance, and cover more than 2,000 hectares. On the vast extent of bare and windswept rock, vegetation is sparse. Here and there, where oak seeds have found a rare patch of shallow soil, stubby oak shrubs struggle to grow. Between the low rock ridges are areas of dank swamp

Scorned by early settlers and farmers, most of it remains Crown land. A century and a half ago, when the few pines in this area were cut away, uncontrolled forest fires burned what little vegetation remained. Rains washed away the unprotected shallow layer of soil.

Although there are no trails, beaches or picnic sites, the Barrens

David Cronenberg filmed a movie at the eerie Torrance Barrens.

are an area through which to walk and to wonder. What Cronenberg-inspired creatures might lurk in so eerie a landscape?

The Southwood Road, Muskoka Road 13, winds through the area between Torrance and Severn Bridge. The Barrens begin south of Highway 169, just across two sets of railway tracks. They continue along the road for a few kilometres, then just as suddenly are gone. Beyond their southern limits is the little pioneer community of Southwood with its historic log church.

The Barrens extend west almost to the waters of Georgian Bay 15 kilometres away. The area has no roads. A few cottages were built on Nine Mile Lake. Other lakes are little more than long thin ponds in the crevices between the empty ridges.

Despite the traffic and the condominiums in the lakes and villages of Muskoka, the Torrance Barrens remain a landscape that the modern world has forgotten, except for David Cronenberg.

# 37

# The Cyprus Lake Grotto

The timeless and irresistible forces of nature sometimes create magical landscapes.

Few people enter a cave to go diving. Yet within the boundaries of one of Canada's newest national parks, the Bruce Peninsula National Park, cave swimmers can dive into waters 12 metres deep. Twenty metres long, the grotto ranges in width from nine to 12 metres, and looks out onto a small cove surrounded by rugged grey cliffs and a beach of broken boulders. Its isolation, its rugged beauty, and the tranquillity of a turquoise blue lagoon, make the setting almost magical.

For tens of thousands of years the waves of Georgian Bay relentlessly pounded away at the limestone cliffs of the Bruce Peninsula. Deep inside, rainwater crept through cracks in the limestone to dissolve the rock from within. The result is a shoreline of cliffs, caves, the unusual rock pillars known as "flowerpots," and the Cyprus Lake Grotto. This outstanding assembly of unusual natural features, along with many rare species of flora and fauna, has long made the Peninsula a popular destination for hikers and naturalists.

Lack of public land has hindered access for most. To remedy this, Parks Canada created a new national park to allow Canadians to experience one of their nation's great natural wonders. Local politics prevented the park from being the entire northern peninsula.

While the Bruce Peninsula has only a small population, enough complained about the "southerners" ruining their life style that the park ended up being only a fraction of its intended size.

Bruce Peninsula National Park consists of only three unconnected segments. The Fathom Five segment is set aside for divers to explore the underwater caves and shipwrecks off the northern Bruce Peninsula. The Flowerpot Island segment contains the best examples of these towering limestone pillars. At the Cyprus Lake segment the grotto is found.

Limestone pillars known as "flowerpots" in Bruce Peninsula National Park.

The shoreline grotto in Bruce Peninsula National Park is popular with visitors.

Many natural features make this little landscape around the grotto appear even more unusual. All along the shoreline, overhanging cliffs, underground passages, natural caves and grottos and dark crevices combine to create a landscape only a few minutes walk from the nearest parking lot.

A trail leads from the "Head of Trails" parking lot beyond the campgrounds, and follows level ground to the shore. Walking becomes more challenging as the trail climbs cliffs and broken boulders. To reach the grotto entrance it is necessary to scramble down a ten-metre cliff, or locate the "hidden" tunnel, a more level approach just back from the shoreline.

The grotto also lies on the world-famous Bruce Hiking Trail, which extends more than 400 kilometres from Tobermory, at the tip of the Bruce Peninsula, to Queenston on the Niagara River. Despite all the local opposition, magical places like the Cyprus Lake grotto can't be kept secret for long.

# Getting It Right

# 38

# The Paintings of Welland, Midland, and Pembroke

In 1978, the citizens of Chemainus, British Columbia, started something when they revitalized their fast fading little town with an outdoor gallery of magnificent murals. The town is now one of BC's leading tourist attractions. In 1985, the tiny Ontario village of Athens, north of Kingston, gained fame with murals of its own. Since then, several communities across the province have depicted their history and heritage on the walls of their downtown buildings. Those in Welland, Midland and Pembroke are among the best.

A mural in downtown Midland depicts busy railway days.

This outdoor mural in downtown Pembroke recalls its history.

In 1990, the Pembroke Heritage Mural Committee unveiled the first murals in this one-time mill town on the banks of the Ottawa River. Drawing on the skills of nearly a dozen artists, among them Stefan Bell, John Ellenberger, and Karole Marois, the committee commissioned almost two dozen murals to date. Concentrated in a six-block area of downtown Pembroke, they depict much of the city's rich heritage. Industries including lumbering, and farming are on a three-panel mural five metres high and more than 30 metres long. Other images include steamboating on the Ottawa River, old-time fiddling and step dancing, and a picture of the city's now-demolished Grand Trunk station.

Transportation, not surprisingly, is a recurring theme among Welland's 29 murals. Several, like Stefan Bell's *Towpaths* and Bas Degroots's *Canal Construction*, depict the story of the Welland Canal, while others, like Ron Baird's *Steam Engine*, recount

Welland's days of rail. Other artists include Risto Turunen, Greg Garand and Andrew Miles. While most of the murals are located along or near the main street, several appear on suburban malls.

In contrast to the many artists who participated in the murals of Pembroke and Welland, the murals of Midland are primarily the work of one man, Fred Lenz, though Dan Sawatzky of Chemainus fame painted two. Born in Germany in 1931, Lenz migrated to Canada in 1951 and soon became one of the country's leading commercial artists. His paintings depict Midland's natural and industrial heritage including nearby Wye Marsh, railway scenes, and Midland's early harbour. Several portray early main street businesses. Most of the 25 murals are concentrated within a six-block area near King Street, the town's main drag.

While Ontario's weak heritage laws cannot protect historic buildings from demolition, many history-minded communities, like Pembroke, Welland and Midland, ensure their remaining buildings contribute to their heritage.

# 39

# Walkerville:
## A Perfect Company Town

Nineteenth century company towns were seldom attractive. They were built in a hurry to offer factory workers crude cheap housing close to the industrial works of their employer. In some cases, workers were paid in chits rather than cash, redeemable only at the company store, which habitually charged exorbitant prices. Workers in U.S. company towns often died broke as Tennessee Ernie Ford put it his hit song, Fifteen Tons, "owing their soul to the company store."

Walkerville, now part of Windsor, was a happy exception. In 1858, shortly after the Great Western Railway reached the shores of

Hiram Walker's company office symbolizes the care put into their company town, Walkerville.

the Detroit River, an American, Hiram Walker, chose Canadian soil to build a distillery. With prohibition in his home state of Michigan, the location would give him access to thirsty customers without running afoul of the law.

The community remained a small industrial village until 1885. Then the Walkers began to expand, incorporating first a railway, the Erie Essex and Detroit River Railway, then adding a furniture factory and a wagon works which evolved into the General Motors Company's Windsor plant.

The town expanded. Rather than develop a cheap looking community, the Walkers hired renowned architect Albert Kahn to design their new office, the family mansion, and many employee homes. The town was thoughtfully laid out along a long thin strip of land, typical of the land lots along the river. The industrial area was close to the river to access not just the railways, but clandestine trans-river

Walkerville's historic downtown contains gardens and preserved buildings.

shipping, another word for smuggling. The family mansion, named Willistead, was built at the south end surrounded by the solid homes of management. Between the two lay the workers' homes, consisting of rowhouses and duplexes, and the small commercial core with a large hotel and bank.

Walkerville developed in two phases. North of Wyandotte Street was the first phase. Here the workers' row houses were built in a Richardsonian Romanesque style. The heavy squat appearance was popular at the time. Streets were laid out in the typical grid pattern. The second phase occurred between Wyandotte and Richmond Streets. Curved streets followed the Garden City approach to city planning. Homes had to be 3,500 square feet.

Unlike the squalid conditions in the dirty company towns of industrial England, or the slave-like conditions in America's mining towns, Walker provided all the amenities. These included street lamps, plumbing, a fire brigade, and free police protection, as well as financing for schools and churches.

For many years the town remained both visually distinctive and strongly independent. Along with neighbouring Ford City, a decidedly less attractive company town, Walkerville was known as one of the Border Cities.

After its incorporation into the City of Windsor in 1935, Walkerville retained its distinctive appearance to this day. The magnificent company offices are designated as a heritage site. Willistead was donated to the City and is now part of a park. The fine old bank and hotel have scarcely been altered. Twenty-seven separate properties in Walkerville have been designated as heritage properties. The entire community is being considered for designation as a heritage district. Although Ontario's weak heritage laws offer no protection against actual demolition, the designation testifies to the unique character of the area and should encourage its preservation.

Historic Walkerville lies between Riverside Drive on the north and Tecumseh Road on the south. Willistead is located on Richmond St. Walking tours have been designed for those wanting to enjoy the flavour of a fine old company town at a leisurely pace.

# 40

# A City for the Birds

High in the hills south of Picton lies a city that is strictly for the birds. Started in 1980s by the Prince Edward Region Conservation Authority, it is literally a city of birdhouses. Not too surprisingly, the 92 birdhouses are called Birdhouse City.

Staff members at the Macaulay Mountain Conservation Area built birdhouses to resemble some of the regions many historic structures such as the courthouse, fire hall, and old churches. Pretty soon, everyone got into the act. Participants in Experience '80 contributed the Paddle wheeler, a police car and a "fly-in" theatre. Others added miniature log cabins, mills and grain elevators: the fire department built a mini-fire hall, while the local McDonalds donated, naturally, a McDonalds "fly-through."

Nor was "city planning" overlooked. The architectural drafting class of Prince Edward Collegiate planned the city. The Lake Ontario Cement Company donated the labour and materials for a centrally located fountain.

Visitors can follow the "flighty" streets with names like "Swallow Hill Road," and see the swallows darting in and out of replicas of the historic Massasauga Park Hotel, a Greek Temple or a Pennsylvania Dutch barn. Robins chirp from the re-creations of the Old White Chapel, a prominent local historic site, the Roblin mill, or the old town hall.

Birds love it. The purple martins, the wrens and the bluebirds flit from cottage to carousel to the thrush bank. When winter comes, most of the residents become 'snow birds.'

Birdhouse City is in the Macaulay Mountain Conservation Area, on County Road 8.

"Empty-nesters" in Picton's Birdhouse City.

# 41

# A Suburb of Last Resort

Where do century-old farmhouses go when urban sprawl engulfs the cornfields? Most fall beneath the wrecker's ball to be replaced by an endless sea of look-alike new homes. But in the heritage-conscious community of Markham, historic houses are given a new lease on life.

Markham, a fast- growing area of big box stores, endless malls, and gridlock traffic, sits of the northeastern fringe of the Greater Toronto Area. Despite unchecked growth, Markham retains much of its built heritage.

That heritage dates back to the 1790s when the area was still covered with a dark forest. In 1794, William Berczy led a group of 64 German families to Canada to be joined later by a number of Pennsylvania Dutch families fleeing the United States. Some established the mill town of German Mills, tucked into the headwaters of the Don River. Others followed the Rouge River to take up farm lots on the most fertile land in Ontario.

While financial failure ruined Berczy and turned German Mills into a ghost town, the farmers prospered. Farm villages and mill towns appeared across the landscape. One of the most successful was Markham. Had it not received a railway station on the Toronto and Nipissing Railway in 1871, it might have remained just another stagnant mill town. But the railways gave

The Town of Markham has a subdivision for historic homes.

it a boost, brought new industries, and a busy main street.

Thanks to Markham's citizens and politicians, much of that heritage has been retained. The historic main street, like the smaller village of Unionville a few kilometres west, has been carefully preserved. New main street development must be compatible with the historic theme. Money from the federal Millennium Fund rescued the 128-year-old railway station from certain demolition.

And then there are the Markham Heritage Estates.

Faced with the loss of countless historic farmhouses and village homes to urban sprawl, the Town of Markham gave the houses a home.

In 1996, Markham created, adjacent to its museum village, a plan of subdivision solely for the purpose of relocating threatened heritage houses. Under the plan, the Town of Markham will sell the lots to owners of heritage homes threatened with demolition at less than market value. The amount saved on the price of the lot provides the owners with the incentive to relocate and restore the houses in the new location.

The plan includes 38 lots. More than half was occupied by the end of 1998.

Among the oldest of the relocated houses are the David Leek House (24 David Gohn Circle) built in 1840 and formerly located in the vanished village of Dollar, and the 1845 house (28 David Gohr Circle) built by Richard Lewis in the community of Gormley.

Although the curving streets look like any other suburb, the handsome homes radiate a genuine aura of history found nowhere else in Ontario. Heritage Corners Lane, the entrance to Markham Heritage Estates, is located on 16th Avenue about 2 kilometres west of Highway 48.

The subdivision's wide streets give the historic community a modern appearance.

# 42

# A Green Sudbury

Could the black barren moonscape described as one of the world's worst environmental disasters be green? American astronauts practiced their moonwalks on the tormented soil. But it is green. In September of 1997, near the famous Big Nickel, the three-millionth tree was planted to mark 19 years of re-greening Sudbury.

A century ago, Sudbury was green. Pine forests covered the granite rocks. In 1883, the Canadian Pacific Railway blasted these rocks to make way for the national dream of a rail line to the Pacific. The discovery of the world's largest deposit of copper and nickel turned the little railway junction into an essential industry. But nickel refining is also of the most polluting industries.

An obsolete process called roasting caused the damage. Crushed ore was laid on vast beds of burning cordwood. The roasting beds burned for months sending billowing clouds of sulphur-laden smoke across the landscape. The smoke killed everything it touched. The refinery stacks were even worse. Tiny particles of nickel and copper oxide seeped into and poisoned the ground.

Trees were killed in all directions. The ground was barren. Nothing grew in the poisoned terrain.

Then, in 1969, when INCO constructed a superstack to spread the fumes further afield, local residents decided o make Sudbury green again. The first efforts at reforestation on the infertile ground

Three million trees have been replanted on what was
once a barren, polluted moonscape.

were dismal failures. A few years later Laurentian University biology professor, Keith Winterhalder, began to experiment with lime. By laying down a layer of limestone first, the poisons were neutralized. Once the grass took hold, the trees followed.

During the mid-70s school children re-greened the moonscapes around their schools. In 1978, the Region of Sudbury successfully tapped into a federal funding program, Young Canada Works. More students worked on a further 70 hectares. By 1983, over 1,200 unemployed miners, funded by all levels of government, as well as Inco and Falconbridge, the area's major mining companies, replanted hillsides and tailings. A decade later more than 25 square kilometres of barren moonscape was green again.

The efforts have won several national and international awards, including the Lieutenant Governor's Conservation Award, the United States Chevron Conservation Award, and the United Nations Local Government Honours Award presented at the Earth Summit in Rio de Janeiro.

In l997, the regional municipality placed a plaque beside its premier landmark, the Big Nickel, announcing the planting of the three-millionth tree. Ironically, looming on the next hill are the cleaned-up Inco stacks. But in between lies a young green forest of saplings that could only be imagined a few years earlier.

Once the area's major polluter, Inco's Sudbury stacks overlook a young forest.

# Transport
# to the Past

# 43

# Toronto's Forgotten
# Carrying Place

To Ontario's first inhabitants, the lakes, rivers, and portages were
the highway. Little survives of Ontario's First Nations' heritage. The
villages were seldom permanent and were moved at frequent intervals. Constructed of wooden long houses within a timber palisade,
their village sites are evident now only to the trained eye of an
archaeologist. Urban development and countryside sprawl have
obliterated many of the native village sites, and the carrying places
that linked them.

Unlike the "portages" across which today's canoeists and
campers carry light-weight tents and two-person canoes around a
few metres of rapids or over a short height of land, Ontario's early
carrying places meant lugging huge freighter canoes over many
miles of difficult terrain. One of the most important of these over-
land routes linked Lake Ontario with Lake Simcoe and was known
as the Toronto Carrying Place. Early French maps show Lake Simcoe as "*Lac du Toronto*," meaning the "place of the fishing weirs."
Remnants of weirs can still be found between Lake Simcoe and Lake
Couchiching.

The Toronto Carrying Place followed the Humber River, (then
the "Toronto River") over the height of land now known as the Oak
Ridge Moraine, and into the Holland River. Along it were a number
of early native villages such as Teiaiagon, now called Baby Point in

A reconstructed Fort Kente at the Quinte Carrying Place.

Etobicoke. At the mouth of the Humber, Jean Rousseau built the Toronto area's first non-native, non-military structure. On this historic site Toronto's City Council recently approved a car wash.

When John Graves Simcoe arrived to set the stage for British settlement, he rejected the Toronto Carrying Plane as a route to the north. Instead, in 1793, he ordered the surveying of Yonge Street. With the opening of this new link to Holland Landing, the Toronto Carrying Place was abandoned.

While Yonge Street has become a busy celebrated urban and suburban corridor, the Toronto Carrying Place is ignored. Were it not for the King Township Historical Society, it might have been forgotten. In 1975, with help from the former Township of King and Town of Vaughan, the society installed historical markers at locations where the carrying place crosses today's roads. The first of a proposed eight markers was unveiled on the King Vaughan Road just west of Mill Road.

Native carrying places have left legacies elsewhere. In Prince Edward County, the community of Carrying Place is named for the portage that crossed the neck of land separating Lake Ontario from the Bay of Quinte. At the western terminus of this portage an early Sulpician mission to the Indians, Fort Kente, has been replicated.

In a few cases, the early carrying places and native trails evolved into paved roads. Toronto's Davenport Road, the Hockley Road, portions of Dundas Street, and the Lakeshore Road, all follow early native trails.

Were it not for efforts like the King Historical Society and Prince Edward County, these historic routes would be forgotten.

Historical markers show the route of the long-abandoned Toronto Carrying Place.

# 44

# In Search of the
## Old Welland Canals

A trivia question would be "How many Welland Canals are there?" Most would say "one": a few more knowledgeable souls might hazard "two." But the correct answer is "four." To find the ruins of the first two goes back to an era when transportation was different than today.

Ground was broken for the first canal in 1824. A narrow ditch with wooden locks followed Twelve Mile Creek from Port Dalhousie to St. Catharines and up the escarpment. From Port Robinson it followed Chippewa Creek to its first terminus at Chippewa on the Niagara River. But it quickly became apparent that both the wooden locks and the route were inadequate.

In 1842, Canal number two began. Open for business in 1851, it replaced the forty wooden locks with 27 stone structures. Industries located near the locks, and with the arrival of the railways, St. Catharines grew. But the designers were too conservative in their predictions of the size of ships and traffic that the canal could handle. In 1872 yet a third canal started.

The new route required only 25 locks. But shipping outgrew the canal. It was obsolete by the time it opened in 1881. Finally in 1913, work started on number four, the Welland Ship Canal. Interrupted by the war, the canal opened in 1933. This time a completely new terminus was built at Port Weller. The mere seven locks were

This abandoned lock from the second canal is one of the steps in a series of locks called Neptune's Staircase.

deepened and twinned to allow more traffic. In 1973, a new bypass was constructed around Welland, giving the canal the current route.

The old routes are for the history buff. The best way to trace the early alignments and to see the old locks is to follow the Merritt Trail in St. Catharines. Two parks provide particularly good opportunities to explore them. Princess Park, along Oakdale Ave., south of Westchester Ave., displays a half dozen stone locks. Gateless but sound, they function now as open sewers.

Near the corner of Bradley Street and Mountain Road is Mountain Locks Park. Some trail users nicknamed it "Neptune's staircase" because a series of seven locks climbs the Niagara Escarpment like a giant staircase. While the upper few locks contain open sewers, the lower ones are ruins in the woods.

Here is the stone ruin of one the canal's earliest industries, the Beaver Cotton Mill, built in the 1860s. Neglected now, it's a roofless ruin collapsed behind a chain link fence. Although for most of the route canal number two was built over number one, for a short distance, they lie side by side. Although number one is little more than a wooded gully, the Welland Canal Society has reconstructed lock 29, and excavated the wooden walls of the long lost first canal. Reach the site by crossing the footbridge near the corner of Christina and Bradley. Follow the trail blazes for about 300 paces. Two of the original lock masters' houses, number 77 and 135 Bradley, are now private homes.

The most remarkable aspect of the locks is their stunning narrowness. Wide enough for a vessel the size of a modern motorboat, they emphasize how slow and arduous transportation was only a century and half ago. While the modern Welland Ship Canal remains a remarkable fixture on the landscape of the Niagara peninsula, only in St. Catharines are extensive remnants of the early canals visible.

A rare lock from the first canal has been excavated and reconstructed.

# 45

# The Thousand Islands Railway

The shorter the railway lines the greater the nostalgia they invoke. A hundred years ago, Ontario boasted a dense network of railway lines.

Many lines were long and ambitious. The Grand Trunk extended from Quebec to Sarnia and Windsor. The Canadian Pacific laid rails across the nation. The patchwork of lines that became the Canadian Northern was a few years away. Many ambitious railways fell far short of their hoped-for destination. The Brockville, Sault Ste. Marie, and Western went only to Westport. The grandly named "James Bay Junction" railway had only miles of track near Parry Sound.

But lines like the Huntsville and Lake of Bays Railway, the London and Port Stanley Railway, and the Thousand Islands Railway wanted to remain short. When water was a key component of Ontario's transportation network, short lines provided a key linkage. The L and PS linked the railways of London with the port on Lake Erie. The HLB portage railway linked steam ship operations on Peninsula Lake and Lake of Bays in Muskoka. The TIR connected the Grand Trunk Railway with the wharves of Gananoque.

The legacy left by such lines varies. The LPS has revived as a tourist train operation called the Port Stanley Terminal Railway. But the Huntsville and Lake of Bays line has left little except equipment

An old engine sits on display in front of Gananoque's little "umbrella" station.

at the Muskoka museum in Huntsville. Although the rails of the Thousand Islands Railway are silent now, much effort has been made to preserve some of its more interesting vestiges.

The Grand Trunk Railway chose a site three kilometres inland to lay its rails and locate a station to avoid an awkward track configuration and higher land costs of Gananoque. In response, the Village of Gananoque incorporated Ontario's shortest railway, the Gananoque and Rideau Railway.

In 1872, construction began. The promoters, however, ran out of money before it could reach the GT. A decade later, the Rathbun Company, builders of the Bay of Quinte Railway, purchased some wharf -side property, and offered to complete the link. On December 14th, 1884, the renamed Thousand Islands Railway opened for business.

From its sprawling wooden wharf station, the line wound through town, passing the dainty little "umbrella" station at King

Street, and along the banks of the Gananoque River to Gananoque Junction. In 1899, as part of its upgrading, the Grand Trunk announced plans for a fine new station with a front tower a mile and half east of the original junction. The TIR continued to use the old junction station, renamed Cheeseborough, until 1934 when it was demolished.

Canadian National Railways took over the GTR in the early 1920s. CNR built an attractive new brick station to accommodate the growing popularity of the Thousands Islands tour boats. Both wharf and junction were busy termini for the TIR. Lumber and coal were shipped from the wharf. The new Junction developed into a little community in its own right. Meanwhile an attractive new masonry station replaced the outdated wooden wharf station.

For four decades the operation remained an institution in the little town. With the arrival of Highway 401 in 1959, and the refusal of the CN to carry "less-than-carload" freight, the days of the TIR were numbered. Passenger service ended in 1962. In 1970 the agent at the junction was removed. In 1986, the track through town was abandoned. In 1997, the entire Gananoque spur fell silent.

Thanks to local historians, much of the TIR has been preserved. The little umbrella station, built by the Rathbuns in 1883, stands beside the former Albion Hotel, which houses a museum. Beside it is the diminutive diesel, number 500, which hauled the solitary passenger coach between the wharf and the junction. The old bridge across the river is now a footbridge. After the wharf station burned in the early 1990s, the entire waterfront was redeveloped, with parks, shops and restaurants. New industrial development at the original junction site obliterated any evidence of its past.

At the "new" junction, the station still stands, though aluminum siding covers up its original features. VIA passenger trains stop twice a day, representing the last active vestige of Gananoque's railway heritage.

# 46

# North America's Longest Streetcar Branch

When a tire manufacturer, a gasoline company and a truck maker conspired during the 1920s and 30s to purchase and shut down the streetcar systems in most American cities, Toronto was spared.

Queen Street in Toronto witnessed North America's second horse-drawn streetcar service in 1861 just three months following the inauguration of the first streetcar on Yonge Street. Between 1892 and 1894, Toronto converted to electric power.

The electric street railways spread along the early pioneer routes that radiated outward from old Toronto: Yonge Street, Dundas, and Kingston Road, partly renamed Queen Street. Commercial development and housing subdivisions followed, and consumed the farm villages.

Buses or subways have replaced most of the streetcar routes. But Dundas, College, King, and Queen Streets remain in operation. The longest and most interesting is Queen Street 501.

From its eastern terminus at the Harris filtration plant to its western reaches in Long Branch, a simple streetcar ride provides a remarkable cross section of the many faces of Toronto. Neighborhoods range from upscale to downtrodden. The car passes taverns, churches and stores that have stood for a century and a half and the vestiges of a dozen villages that existed before the city expanded past them.

Streetcar 501 loops at the western terminus of North America's longest streetcar line.

The ride begins in the "Beaches" or, more correctly, the "Beach." Once a beach side recreational destination, the area was dominated by large estates, tiny cottages, and amusement parks. Streetcars arrived jammed with holidayers. But as the city grew, most of the estates and amusement parks became housing lots. The area evolved into an upscale residential community.

At the Neville Loop, the route's eastern terminus, is the remarkable art deco architecture of the R.C. Harris filtration plant. Built between 1932 and 1955 the plant is on the site of the popular Victoria Park amusement ground. As it traverses the Beach, the streetcar passes a lengthy and eclectic array of trendy shops and restaurants. Kew Gardens, originally a private amusement park operated by Joseph Williams, is the geographic focus of the Beach, and the site of the many musical festivals.

At Woodbine Avenue, the western limits of the Beach, a massive new housing development occupies the site of the historic landmark the Greenwood racetrack. West of Coxwell Ave. the streetcar enters the one-time village of Leslieville. The 1840s Ashbridge house is to the north. To the south, Laing Avenue has its controversial maple tree which many claim inspired Alexander Muir, then a local school principal, to write the *Maple Leaf Forever.*

The route then passes beneath the CN railway bridge that marks the easterly limit of the community of Donmount. Historic brick stores, columned one-time banks and the once handsome hotel that dominates the corner of Broadview date from the earliest days of streetcar service. The streetcar then crosses over the channelized Don River and into the area of lower Cabbagetown. An area where gentrification meets the poor of society, upscale lofts in the historic Queen Street Brewery are just down the street from Toronto's most frequented soup kitchens.

Between there and Toronto's main artery, Yonge Street, the route leads through one of the oldest sections of town, Old York. In 1793, the first ten city blocks were laid out for what would become, in less than two centuries, the largest city in Canada. The most prominent building of the era still standing on Queen St., is the Metropolitan United Church at the corner of Church Street.

"Downtown" Toronto has traditionally been the corner of Queen and Yonge. Here the country's two retailing giants, Eatons and Simpsons faced off across the street from each other. While the old Eaton's store was replaced by the ill-planned but popular Eaton's Centre, the elegant Simpsons store stands on the south west corner, now restored and a part of The Bay retail chain.

Between Yonge St. and Spadina comes institutional Toronto. "Old" City Hall, built during the 1880s on the north east corner of Queen and Bay, stands next to the distinctive clam-shaped "new" city hall, built in 1966. At University Avenue, the city's most historic structure, the Osgoode Hall law school, dates from the 1830s. The odd looking wrought iron gate was designed to keep out the cattle that wandered the nearby fields at the time.

The character of Queen Street changes yet again between University and Bathurst. Alternative clothing stores and gothic comic shops are dominated by the popular CHUM/CITY TV building. Housed in a 1913 terra-cotta-clad former site of Ryerson Publishers at the southeast corner of Queen and John, the TV studio is the site of outdoor rock sessions, and the popular "Speaker's Corner."

At the north east corner of Soho is one of Queen Street's oldest buildings. The oldest portion of the Black Bull tavern was built in 1833. Meanwhile, the interesting red building at 280 Queen will be familiar to fans of the CBC *Street Legal* series as the building that housed the law offices of the lead characters.

Spadina Avenue shows a decidedly distinctive character. The wide roadway recalls its role as the boulevard to the Spadina mansion far to the north. Streetcar service has recently been re-introduced onto Spadina where the jumble of red and yellow store signs reflects the growing number of Chinese and Vietnamese merchants.

Beyond Bathurst, Queen Street reverts to its roots. Here is a Mecca for used clothing stores, family run shops, and rough and tumble taverns. The heart of Parkdale was once the old Parkdale railway station. It was located on the south side of the street where the streetcar passes beneath the long limestone underpass. Though it burned in the late 1960s, the 1889 Gladstone Hotel, which stood opposite the station, has been refurbished as one of the most elegant buildings on this section of Queen Street.

At Roncesvalles, the landscape again changes abruptly. Gone is the old city. The streetcar route glides down a gentle grade and follows the lakeshore to the site of the Sunnyside Amusement Park. The only reminders of those slower times are the Palais Royale and the columned swimming pool. A large forested estate follows the tracks on the north side. John Howard donated High Park to the city in 1873. His historic Colborne Lodge, supposedly haunted, still stands and serves as a museum. Within the park is Grenadier Pond, named after the drowning of three soldiers from the early garrison

Again, the landscape changes quickly as the streetcar slips under a railway bridge and enters the community of Mimico. Solid homes and small apartment buildings back right onto Lake Ontario.

Mimico Avenue leads north from what is here called Lakeshore Road. The avenue was the community's first main street when it was little more than a railway village, far out in the country, with a station, hotel, and a small number of stores.

Lakeshore Road widens noticeably through the extensive commercial strip that marks New Toronto. Laid out as an industrial and railway town, the rigid grid of streets are not named, but rather numbered from First Street all the way to 43rd Street. Islington Ave., which was once 7th Street, marks the core of the community. Near Kipling Ave., the route passes the grounds of the former Mimico Lunatic Asylum. These remarkable century-old buildings, many empty, have been designated as an historic district, owned now by Seneca College.

New Toronto merges almost imperceptibly into Long Branch, a much older community. In the 1870s, when Toronto was little more than a pall of haze on the horizon, Long Branch developed as a summer retreat with a hotel and a row of lakeside cottages. Later, with the arrival of the streetcars, most were converted to permanent homes, or replaced outright.

At this point the streetcar swings into the loop at the Long Branch station. The oldest streetcar shelter still in use in the system marks the termination of Route 501. From here, the lake, and the old cottages are about a 10-minute walk.

While the trip can take over an hour, the best way to enjoy this unusual route is to buy an inexpensive day pass that allows unlimited stop-offs. The streetcar on North America's longest streetcar branch is the simplest way to sample the faces of old Toronto.

# 47

# Pakenham's Bridge

Among Ontario's heritage features, bridges are the least appreci-
ated. Yet Ontario boasts many distinctive bridges. North America's
longest wooden bridge crosses Sioux Narrows in northwestern
Ontario. West Montrose, near Kitchener, is the only remaining covered bridge in Ontario. A railway swing bridge provides the only
road access to Manitoulin, the world's largest freshwater island.

One of the most beautiful of Ontario's bridges is Pakenham's
Bridge, the only five-span stone arched bridge in North America.

Built in 1901, it replaced a rickety wooden structure. The bridge
was so unsafe it was illegal to cross "at a faster pace than a walk."
Designed by the firm of O'Toole and Keating, the 85-metre bridge
is made up of five 15-metre stone arches on piers that are three
metres thick. The huge stones for the bridge were dragged from a
nearby quarry. The largest stone is three metres long by nearly a
metre square, and weighs five tonnes.

In 1984, Ontario's Ministry of Transportation, along with the
Ontario Heritage Foundation, and Ottawa's National Capital Commission, restored the bridge, inserting reinforced concrete into the
deck and parapet walls in the stonework

Pakenham village itself is also worth a visit. Despite its location
well inland from Ontario's first towns and villages, Pakenham got
off to an early start. By 1831 it had become the site of a sawmill,

With its five stone arches, the Pakenham Bridge is the only one of its kind in North America.

store and post office, and was named Little Falls. In 1840 Andrew Dickson sold the first village lots. Just twenty years later the village claimed a population of 800. Despite getting the railway in the 1880s, Pakenham failed to grow. The population is about the same today which helped preserve its rich heritage.

On the main street, only a short distance from the bridge, are such historic buildings as the Byrne Home Hardware, housed in a mid-1800s classic revival building, Paddye Mann Designs in an 1830s stone building, and Ontario's "oldest" general store. Built in 1840 the Pakenham general store contains crafts, memorabilia, freshly baked breads, as well as the usual range of grocery items. On the opposite side of the bridge, the Stone Bridge Shop operates from a converted 1842 stone gristmill.

Pakenham is on Highway 15 about halfway between Almonte and Arnprior, and about 60 kilometres west of downtown Ottawa. Caution should be used if crossing the bridge on foot: there is no sidewalk, the roadway is narrow, and County Road 20 can be busy.

# Mining Days

# 48

# Hemlo Gold

To the untrained eye, the tiny specks circled with a red wax pen on the core samples look like anything but a major gold find. Most gold lovers expect a nugget that suddenly appears in the waters of a rushing stream or a golden vein in a chunk of quartz.

No one paid much attention to the Hemlo deposit until the 1970s. Although gold deposits were known to exist between White River and Marathon since the last century, the gold seekers were looking for nuggets not specks. In the 1970s, a Thunder Bay geologist concluded that although the golden specks were small, they occurred with enough regularity over such a vast area that the deposit was as valuable as legendary Klondike or the Porcupine gold fields. By the 1980s three gold mining companies were fighting, two of them in court, to dig and reap the riches.

The extensive and predictable distribution of the golden specks made the deposit easier to extract. Huge quantities of ore are crushed into powder and the gold is melted and chemically separated. Even though every tonne of ore crushed yields only a microscopic quarter ounce of gold, as long as the price of gold remains above $150 US per ounce, the Hemlo gold fields will remain among the most profitable in the world.

More than geological configuration makes the gold field so striking. All three operations are beside the Trans Canada Highway, within metres of each other. To the Trans Canada traveler, used to endless bush, punctuated only by the wasteful clear-cut of the pulp companies, the modern head frames suddenly looming above the treetops are a visual shock.

The one thing missing are the boomtowns that normally huddle around the shafts, or are strung out along the roads. In a rare attempt at sound land use planning, the Ontario government ordered all new growth would occur only in existing towns. The infrastructure either already existed, or could be expanded, to accommodate the boom. Most was directed to the odorous pulp mill town of Marathon scenically situated on the shore of Lake Superior. The rest went to inland Manitouwadge while a smaller portion was allocated to White River. The neat new subdivisions with modern houses and curving streets will disappoint those looking for the ramshackle boomtowns of old.

But in forty years, when the deposits are expected to run out, or sooner if gold prices drop much further, the mines will fall silent, as all mines do. And the boomtowns will then take on the aura of the ghost towns that are found around so many other expired mines.

Modern headframes of Canada's richest gold field loom beside the Trans Canada Highway.

# 49

# Marmora's Big Hole

The huge pit may become Ontario's biggest swimming pool. As each year passes, the huge open pit left by the Marmaraton Iron Mine fills with a little more water. Though nobody will be swimming in it any day soon, it makes for one of Ontario's most unusual mining sights.

Mining days in Marmora date back to 1820. An iron magnate named Charles Hayes hacked a trail through the dark forests of central Hastings, hundreds of miles from the nearest city of any size. Here he began the construction of a mine, mill and smelter for the production of iron. The community of Marmora quickly grew to a population of 200.

For a time Marmora, and its neighbour Blairton, now a ghost town, were the leading iron producers in the country. Difficulty in transporting the iron out proved their undoing. When canals were completed along the St. Lawrence River cheaper iron could be imported and Marmora's iron mining days were over. Almost.

In 1949 an aeromagnetic survey by the federal and provincial governments revealed strange magnetic anomalies just east of town. Drilling quickly followed and revealed an immense body of ore 2,000 feet long and 400 feet deep. The only difficulty was that 130 feet of limestone lay on top of it.

In 1951 Bethlehem Steel Company of the U.S. began to haul

This mammoth open pit at Marmora is gradually filling with water.

away the intervening rock. The company was soon removing one million tons of magnetic ore every year. CN trains hauled it to the company's steel plant in Lackawanna New York where it was concentrated and pelletized.

But the late 1970s exhausted the ore. The legacy of the closed mine was a massive circular pit a third of a kilometre across and fully 200 metros deep. During the mine's operation, a viewing area was provided so that the public could watch the monster trucks grind up out of the gaping hole loaded with ore. Today, although unmaintained and overgrown, that same observation area allows the same view. Although the huge hole is slowly filling with water, the tailings provide material for crushed stone.

The road to the viewing area leads south of Highway 7 1.4 kilometres east of the traffic lights in Marmora. Although nearly a century and a half older, the site of Marmora's first iron works still exists just north of the intersection, where historic plaques and short walking trails mark the ruins of Ontario's first iron furnace.

# 50

# The Rock Hound Paradise of Bancroft

The Highlands of Hastings are a little known gem in more ways than one. Located midway between Toronto and the upper reaches of the Ottawa Valley, and southeast of Algonquin Park, this region contains southern Ontario's most magnificent mountains and its richest mineral deposits. No where in North America do as many different minerals occur as they do in the Hastings Highlands.

Why one area would have such a singular concentration of mineral deposits has long baffled geologists. A billion and half years ago, a range of mountains as high as the Rockies covered the highlands. A series of cataclysmic upheavals and volcanic activity sent molten lava seeping into crevices. Ordinary rocks became glittering crystals and shimmering minerals.

By the turn of century, the Bancroft area was alive with crude little mines perched on nearly every mineral deposit. Some, like feldspar, talc, mica and graphite, were mined for their industrial use. Others like quartz, garnet, sodalite and marble, were as prized for their beauty and their utility. Most of the deposits, however, were small, and the mines short-lived. Only a few, like Craigmont and Burgess, were large enough to support towns. Today these sites are ghost towns. Most were small camps with head frame, boarding house, and perhaps a processing mill.

Although the deposits outlived their economic usefulness,

An ore cart sits in front of the Bancroft Chamber of Commerce.

Bancroft has a new breed of treasure-seeking prospector, the rock hound.

These intrepid collectors prowl the banks of rivers and hillsides looking for the perfect crystal. As a result the area hosts an annual gathering of like-minded pickers at a festival called the Rockhound

Gemboree. The largest of its kind in the continent, the Gemboree brings the rock hunters early every August to swap, buy, sell, or just scour the hillsides.

To help them along, the local Chamber of Commerce published the Mineral Collecting Guidebook, a common sense guide to nearly 30 collecting sites. True neophytes can turn to a geologist who leads twice weekly excursions from the Chamber of Commerce offices (housed in the former railway station) into the hills, offering insight on how to identify and collect the area's minerals. Several private sites are also open to collectors, such as Beryl Pit, the Bear Lake Diggings, and the Princess Sodalite Mine, one of the rare sodalite deposits outside of South Africa.

The "capital" of the area is the little town of Bancroft. In the hills that surround it are not just the rocks and the minerals, but rugged bush farms, scenic vistas, and pioneer villages little changed since the first settlers arrived over a century ago.

Bancroft lies about two hours' drive from Peterborough along Highway 28, and about an hour north of Highway 7 on Highway 62.

## Answer to the Bean cryptogram on page 77

*Starting from the letter "I", read in a zig-zag counter-clockwise circle and the following dedication appears:*

"In memoriam Henrietta, 1st wife of S.Bean, M.D., who died 27th Sep 1865 aged 23 years 2 months & 17 days & Susanna his second wife who died 27th April 1867 aged 26 years 3 months and 15 days. 2 better wives 1 man never had. They were gifts from God and are now in Heaven May God help me S.B. to meet them there."